WHAT YOUR COLLEAGUES A

What I most love about *How to Deal With Parents Who Are Angry, Troubled, Afraid, or Just Seem Crazy* is Elaine McEwan-Adkins' ability to focus on what really matters. A must-read for both experienced and novice teachers who are looking for a practical resource that gets to the heart of how to create positive partnerships with parents.

—**Chandra Williams**, EdD
CEO, Center for Student Achievement Solutions

Nobody writes a book for educators better than Dr. Elaine McEwan-Adkins. *How to Deal With Parents Who Are Angry, Troubled, Afraid, or Just Seem Crazy* is a commonsensical, go-to handbook for teachers, rich in data and anecdotes to inspire and guide difficult interactions with parents. Buy a copy for every teacher you know!

—**Lydia M. Zuidema**
Director of Academic Development, Office of School Operations
Oasis International Schools

Once again Elaine McEwan-Adkins has captured the essence and wisdom from her own experiences, as well as those of other educators, in dealing with angry parents. The information and stories shared on these pages are sure to help that beginning teacher avoid pitfalls and help them be well prepared for that unexpected or expected confrontational parent. Knowing what to do in advance can help avoid making an enemy, and perhaps make a friend of the angry parent instead. I loved the "What did the teacher learn from this experience?" feature after each story shared by the teachers! This book will be a wonderful resource for new teachers, as well as all educators.

—**Lola Malone**
Retired Educator (Teacher and Principal)
Springdale, AR

With a perfect balance of humor, examples (personal and from others), and concrete, practical advice that focuses on being proactive rather than reactive, Elaine McEwan-Adkins expertly guides teachers to finding satisfying solutions to even the most unpleasant "close encounters of the parental kind."

—**Allyson Burnett**
Director of Professional Learning for Sibme
Adjunct Professor, University of Houston Downtown
Co-Author, *20 Literacy Strategies to Meet the Common Core*

A must read for veteran and novice teachers to understand and respond to the angry, troubled, afraid, or just a little crazy parent. This book looks at the feelings and emotions that parents bring with them and offers a fresh perspective that provides valuable tips to ultimately diffuse the anger and work toward amicable solutions to best serve the student.

—**Salli Mahaffy,** Principal
Bayer Private School, Glendale, AZ

Difficult parents got you down? Then grab hold of this book and breathe easy. You will find authentic scenarios depicting the dysfunctional behaviors that problem parents present, proactive strategies and insightful solutions that build productive parent-teacher relationships, and easy-to-access intervention charts and lists. Elaine McEwan-Adkins may have broken the "be nice" rule with her honest portrayal of disagreeable parents, but the interventions presented will not only support teachers but parents as well.

—**Cathie E. West,** Author of *The Educator's Guide to Writing a Book*

HOW TO DEAL WITH PARENTS WHO ARE

ANGRY,

TROUBLED,

AFRAID,

OR JUST SEEM CRAZY

TEACHERS' GUIDE

HOW TO DEAL WITH PARENTS WHO ARE
ANGRY,
TROUBLED,
AFRAID,
OR JUST SEEM CRAZY

Elaine K.
McEWAN-ADKINS

FOR INFORMATION:

Corwin

A SAGE Company

2455 Teller Road

Thousand Oaks, California 91320

(800) 233-9936

www.corwin.com

SAGE Publications Ltd.

1 Oliver's Yard

55 City Road

London EC1Y 1SP

United Kingdom

SAGE Publications India Pvt. Ltd.

B 1/I 1 Mohan Cooperative Industrial Area

Mathura Road, New Delhi 110 044

India

SAGE Publications Asia-Pacific Pte. Ltd.

18 Cross Street #10-10/11/12

China Square Central

Singapore 048423

Acquisitions Editor: Ariel Curry

Development Editor: Desirée A. Bartlett

Associate Content
Development Editor: Jessica Vidal

Production Editor: Melanie Birdsall

Copy Editor: Cate Huisman

Typesetter: C&M Digitals (P) Ltd.

Proofreader: Theresa Kay

Indexer: Molly Hall

Cover Designer: Scott Van Atta

Graphic Designer: Mackenzie Lowry

Marketing Manager: Margaret O'Connor

Printed in the United States of America

Library of Congress Cataloging-in-Publication Data

Names: McEwan-Adkins, Elaine K., author.

Title: How to deal with parents who are angry, troubled, afraid, or just seem crazy: teachers' guide / Elaine K. McEwan-Adkins.

Description: Thousand Oaks, California: Corwin, [2020] | Includes bibliographical references and index.

Identifiers: LCCN 2019016378 | ISBN 9781544352442 (pbk.: alk. paper)

Subjects: LCSH: Parent-teacher relationships—United States. | Home and school—United States. | Education—Parent participation—United States. | Parents—United States—Psychology.

Classification: LCC LC226.6 .M345 2020 | DDC 371.19/20973—dc23

LC record available at https://lccn.loc.gov/2019016378

This book is printed on acid-free paper.

SFI label applies to text stock

19 20 21 22 23 10 9 8 7 6 5 4 3 2 1

CONTENTS

PREFACE

Several decades and numerous jobs in education have sped by since I was hired for my first teaching assignment, a fifth-grade classroom at an elementary school in a western suburb of Chicago. There were many highlights and some memorable lowlights during that year. There were 35 students in the class that included 5 rambunctious boys who seemingly met after school to craft plans for how to disrupt instruction the next day. My teammate in the classroom next door specialized in off-color jokes and celebrated the holidays with an aborted attempt to kiss me under the fake mistletoe. I couldn't swear that he hadn't sipped some spiked punch.

I handled the crowded classroom and the lecherous old man next door with very little difficulty. The rambunctious boys were handily dealt with when I petitioned the principal to gather all of the available parents (mothers and fathers) together for an evening meeting and requested that she attend and back me up on my "discipline plan." She agreed and we moved forward to lower the boom on this merry band of bad boys. God bless my principal for standing up for me. Every family was represented, and none of the parents who attended the evening meeting were angry. They were grateful that someone was actually doing something to rein in their naughty children and promised to back up my plan, which required that during the first week there would always be someone available to pick up their son at school if he crossed the line I had drawn in the sand.

I didn't run into my first truly angry parent until the November parent-teacher conferences. I can still replay that conference in my brain complete with surround sound and Technicolor. The surround sound was provided by an irate father incensed that I gave his son a C in math. He accused me of standing in the way of this charming child getting into dental school. The Technicolor vividly displayed both his explosively red face and the blotchy blush of humiliation and embarrassment that spread over my face and ears and down my neck. I barely got through that conference with my dignity intact. I think I remained calm and offered some suggestions for how Jake could bring his grade up for the next marking period. I think I suggested that we have a parent-teacher-student conference and bring Jake in on whatever plan we thought might work. I also made a note to myself to carefully monitor Jake's assignment completion, and if he was failing to hand in just one assignment or got less than an A- on his math tests to notify his parents immediately. I didn't have the nerve to tell Jake's dad that his work habits and unwillingness to do homework would be more likely to keep him out of dental school than would a C in math when he was 10 years old. After that day, I vowed to purchase a dozen turtlenecks to wear in advance of parent conferences. The turtlenecks would also come in handy when my teammate launched into another round of bad jokes. Thankfully I have outgrown both my blushes and blotches.

In the years that followed my encounter with Jake's dad, my meetings with parents who were angry, troubled, afraid, or just plain crazy would become commonplace. I no longer developed sweaty palms, a racing heart, and blotchy skin. I became a confident teacher and eventually a "prepared for any eventuality" administrator who had acquired the skills to calm the angriest and to counsel the most troubled. In the pages ahead, I'll share the strategies that have helped me deal with out-of-control parents and introduce you to a variety of experienced contributing teachers who will share their own experiences and advice. You will learn how to emerge unscathed from those "close encounters of the parental kind," and even find yourself enjoying the satisfaction that comes from finding solutions to difficult parental problems.

IMPORTANT WORDS AND THEIR MEANINGS

The title of this book is an intriguing one that resonates for teachers. There are some rare objections to the term *crazy* that have come from individuals who both work in mental health fields *and* have never been classroom teachers. The mental health professionals were concerned, and rightly so, with the stigma attached to the word *crazy* when applied to individuals with mental illness. However, the term never fails to attract the attention of educators who have been verbally or even physically assaulted by parents who were totally out of control.

Let me hasten to explain that my use of the term *crazy* is somewhat tongue in cheek; it specifically refers to irrational and often explosive behavior that is upsetting to others—whatever the cause. Parents can of course be angry, troubled, and afraid without being irrational. In fact, there are dozens of situations that demand a strong dose of righteous indignation. However, when parent behavior crosses the line from being assertive and appropriate to being dangerous, hostile, demeaning, threatening, manipulative, or aggressive, it not only becomes "crazy" but also tends to make educators a little "crazy" themselves.

I wish to be sensitive to my colleagues, friends, and family members who are dealing with depression and anxiety and any other disorders of which I am not aware, and I intend no offense or prejudice. While writing this book, I have come to prefer the term *dysfunctional.* There are many things that can be described as dysfunctional—families, bodily systems, and interpersonal relationships. Dysfunctional parents as described in this book can and do fall into all of the categories set forth in the book's title. What these various types of dysfunctional parents have in common is this: the inability to function in somewhat normal and predictable ways. Their own needs, insecurities, quirky personalities, and mental health diagnoses make forming positive relationships with them almost impossible in some cases. Recent teacher surveys conducted by Corwin have indicated an intense interest by newer teachers in how they can more effectively deal with difficult parents. However, there are many audiences who will benefit from the advice and strategies found in the book.

WHO THIS BOOK IS FOR

I have written this book for the following audiences:

- Newer teachers for whom traditional teacher training has provided little background information or practical strategies for dealing with difficult parents
- Prospective teachers who are in preservice programs
- Experienced classroom teachers who struggle with developing the personal confidence and appropriate interpersonal strategies they need to become well-rounded teachers who can deal with difficult parents
- All teachers who need more specialized information as preparation for attending and participating in IEP meetings and annual reviews with parents
- Principals and teacher mentors who need resources to support novice teachers as they face difficult conferences and interactions with parents
- College and university instructors of teacher-training courses who wish to introduce prospective teachers to the challenges of interacting positively with diverse parent communities

OVERVIEW OF THE CONTENTS

Chapter 1 describes the five facets of today's education landscape that can interact in potentially explosive ways to create an epidemic of angry parents: (1) the increasing variety of today's family units; (2) the needs, issues, and problems of today's students; (3) a continuum of types of schools ranging from those that are highly effective to those that are low performing and close to failing; (4) the all-too-human but totally inappropriate things that teachers do that irritate and inflame parents; and (5) nearly a dozen categories of parental types, all of whom can become angry and distressed at a moment's notice.

Chapter 2 contains more than two dozen tips to implement proactively. They will help you get out ahead of parent problems. Implementing just one or two of the tips and consistently following through with them from the beginning of the school year to the end will make an amazing difference in your relationships with parents.

As proactive as you may be, however, there will always be parents who defy all of your efforts and break all of the rules. For these parents, you need something more substantive. Chapter 3 contains a variety of responsive strategies for defusing parents who are angry, troubled, afraid, or just seem crazy. This chapter will help you to ease the fears, calm the troubled spirits, and shut down the angry outbursts of parents so that you can move to exploring what the problem is and coming up with an action plan to solve it in Chapter 4.

Chapter 4 explains numerous helpful exploratory and action strategies, including a seven-step problem-solving process to help ensure quick solutions to the problems that worry and trouble parents.

In Chapter 5 some experienced educators describe their most memorable angry-parent encounters and then ask and answer the question you should always ask yourself after a traumatic meeting with a parent: *What can I learn from this experience?*

Chapter 6 contains a set of tools and tips to guide you in putting your best self forward as you deal with a variety of types of challenging parents. It will remind you of the importance of continuing to grow and develop your best self.

The Conclusion summarizes the book and enumerates 10 goals that, when achieved, will guarantee your success as a highly effective teacher who can handle every parent problem with a calm, caring approach.

ACKNOWLEDGMENTS

A special thank you to the contributing educators who shared their stories and advice for this book. I am especially grateful to Melanie Birdsall. Over the past two decades, Melanie has taken my words and made them look good on the printed page. I am thrilled that she stepped aside from her supervisory position to shepherd this book to its publication. My books have come a long way from one of my very first Corwin books published in 1998, *The Principal's Guide to Raising Reading Achievement.* In Corwin's early days, covers were simple watercolor washes. My book was purple and became somewhat famous in administrative circles because they could always find it on their shelves. They only needed to look for the purple book.

I have written more than two dozen books for Corwin, but this book is unique. It is the only one that my now deceased husband, Ray Adkins, didn't read, edit, and read several more times to ensure that it was my best work. He zealously cared about what I wrote. He always landed on every spelling and grammar error, but his best editing featured pointing out where my train of thought might have fallen off the tracks.

Ray died February 19 in the Casas de la Luz Hospice in Tucson, Arizona, at the age of 91. He faced two major health challenges in his final years: Alzheimer's and blindness. I cared for him at home with the help of an aide. Ray no longer remembered my books, nor could he recall the hundreds of wonderful trips we took around the country doing workshops and professional development for principals and teachers.

Those of you who met and knew Ray will be comforted to know there were several important things about him that did not change as his disease progressed. He was still the sweet, kind, and generous man who once took care of all of the critical details of our presentations and took time to chat with you during breaks and lunch. He still had a wonderful sense of humor. He still loved me deeply and told me so frequently. Most important, he still retained his great faith and deep spirituality. I dedicate this book to him with profound appreciation for his sense of adventure that motivated both of us to take early retirement, pack up a few treasured pieces of furniture into a big yellow Ryder truck, and drive across the country from the Chicago suburbs to the Sonoran Desert in Oro Valley, Arizona. Ray was most definitely "the wind beneath my wings."

PUBLISHER'S ACKNOWLEDGMENTS

Corwin gratefully acknowledges the contributions of the following reviewers:

Jason Eitner
Superintendent of Schools
Waterford Township School District
Mt. Laurel, NJ

Mitzi Mack
Middle School Media Specialist
Young Middle Magnet School
Tampa, FL

Nina Orellana
Title 1 and Multi-Tiered System of Support (MTSS) Coordinator
Palm Bay Academy Charter School
Palm Bay, FL

Stephanie Turner
Fourth-Grade Teacher, All Subjects, Team Lead
Bradley Academy, An Arts Integrated School
Murfreesboro, TN

ABOUT THE AUTHOR

Elaine K. McEwan-Adkins is an educational consultant with The McEwan-Adkins Group, offering professional development for educators to assist them in meeting the challenges of literacy learning in grades preK–6. A former teacher, librarian, principal, and assistant superintendent for instruction in several suburban Chicago school districts, Elaine is the award-winning and best-selling author of more than three dozen books for educators. Her Corwin titles include *Raising Reading Achievement in Middle and High Schools: Five Simple-to-Follow Strategies for Principals* (2nd ed., 2006), *Seven Strategies of Highly Effective Readers: Using Cognitive Research to Boost K–8 Achievement* (2004), *Ten Traits of Highly Effective Principals: From Good to Great Performance* (2003), *Making Sense of Research: What's Good, What's Not, and How to Tell the Difference* (2003), *Seven Steps to Effective Instructional Leadership,* (2nd ed., 2003), *Teach Them ALL to Read: Catching the Kids Who Fall Through the Cracks* (2002), and *Ten Traits of Highly Effective Teachers: How to Hire, Mentor, and Coach Successful Teachers* (2001).

Elaine was honored by the Illinois Principals Association as an outstanding instructional leader, by the Illinois State Board of Education with an Award of Excellence in the Those Who Excel program, and by the National Association of Elementary School Principals as the National Distinguished Principal from Illinois for 1991. She received her undergraduate degree in education from Wheaton College and advanced degrees in library science (MA) and educational administration (EdD) from Northern Illinois University.

CHAPTER 1

WHY ARE THERE SO MANY ANGRY PARENTS?

Seek first to understand, before you seek to be understood.

—Stephen Covey (1989, p. 235)

If you have a strong desire to work collaboratively with difficult and dysfunctional parents to advance the goals of academic and social success for their children, you will need to understand the variety of variables and their complexities that can often interact explosively to create parents who are angry, troubled, fearful, or just plain dysfunctional. Dealing with difficult parents can be challenging for the most experienced teachers, but it's always on the minds of novice faculty members. In addition to dealing with parents, they are also expected to assimilate new curricula, implement complex technologies, and teach students with a wide range of abilities to master the core curriculum of their grade level or subject specialty.

At first glance, the problem posed by most upset parents would seem to be a relatively straightforward one to solve. First, examine the list of things that teachers do to irritate and inflame parents; second, help teachers to be more sensitive to these issues and encourage them to stop doing them; and finally, provide teachers with some strategies for ameliorating the super sticky situations. What complicates the angry parents problem is that there are more aggravating variables in the angry parents dilemma than just one generic parent and one generic teacher. A *variable* is "a characteristic, number, or quantity that increases or decreases over time, or takes different values in different situations" (Variable, n.d.).

In the dealing with an angry parents scenario, there are five facets, each one with a broad range of variables: (1) the increasing variety of today's *family units*; (2) the range of abilities, needs, issues, and problems of today's *students*; (3) a continuum of types of *schools* ranging from those that are highly effective to those that are low-performing and quite a few that are on their way to failing; (4) the wide variety of all too human, but totally inappropriate, behaviors that *teachers* display that irritate and inflame parents; and (5) nearly a dozen categories of *parent* types who can all become angry and distressed at a moment's notice.

FACET 1: THE INCREASING VARIETY OF TODAY'S FAMILY UNITS

Your natural inclination might be to think of today's parents in terms of the family in which you were raised or even your current family configuration. However, today's students have complicated and often shifting family structures that may have little in common with your experiences. A Pew Research study reported that in 2014, less than half (46%) of U.S. children younger than 18 lived in a traditional home with two married heterosexual parents in their first marriage. Contrast that to 1960, when 73% of children fit that description (Livingston, 2014). Flip the calendar forward to 2017 to tease out another demographic data point: the percentage of children living with an unmarried parent. A 2017 Pew Research study found that this percentage has doubled since 1968, going from 13% then to 32% in 2017 (Livingston, 2018).

These demographics describe today's families in broad strokes. As a teacher you will be expected to map names, faces, personalities, and family dynamics on your students and then proceed to teach to the academic strengths and weaknesses of those students.

Bear in mind that the individuals who show up for the first open house or parent-teacher conference will present to you in many combinations and permutations. You're safest if you wait for the "parental units" to introduce themselves. They might come in the form of grandparents, two mothers, two fathers, an aunt and uncle, a mom and her boyfriend, a father and his girlfriend, foster parents, or even a noncustodial parent who wants to stay connected to a child. Sorting out the demographics of the students you have been assigned for any given school year is an essential part of getting to know "parents" and then enlisting them as members of your team.

Contributing educator Joelle Wright is something of an expert on communicating and meeting the needs of a wide variety of parental units. During her 14 years as a classroom teacher, she has encountered all of the sets of "parents" displayed in Figure 1.1, The Increasing Variety of Today's Family Units, on the following page.

As you consider the variety of today's family units, you can readily see dozens of complicating variables at work. Many of today's family units have enough moving parts to keep both you and your students wondering who's in charge at home. For example, consider the challenges of meeting with a pair of angry grandparents who have adopted their grandchild and are truly unprepared to be parents a second time around. They are struggling with the constant barrage of notes to sign and demands for assistance with homework, to say nothing of navigating social media, email, and the class website. One of the main characters in their "story" is a daughter who has lost custody of her daughter because of mental health and addiction issues. So, in addition to parenting a second time, the grandparents are bearing a load of guilt over their failure to be better parents to their "first" daughter.

FACET 2: THE RANGE OF NEEDS, ISSUES, AND PROBLEMS OF TODAY'S STUDENTS

The students of today present with a wide range of needs, issues, and problems. Figure 1.2, Typology of Today's Students, sets forth and briefly describes each category (see page 5). All of these types of students can be found in almost every type of school.

Contributing educator Joelle Wright notes,

I think it is safe to say that the generation of students we currently have are harder to teach than when I first began teaching 14 ago. There is a distinct increase in the population of students with traumatic backgrounds. Some of these students are now in foster care homes, are living with relative caregivers, or have been adopted. These kids are still struggling, but they have parents who are actively working

FIGURE 1.1   The Increasing Variety of Today's Family Units

Parental Unit	Additional Information
Grandparents who have legally adopted a child	Even though these individuals are the biological grandparents, they are called mom and dad by the child.
Grandparents who are foster parents or have guardianship of their grandchildren	The child refers to these "foster parents" as grandma and grandpa.
Caregivers can also include aunts and uncles or distant relatives that are providing foster care for a child who is related to them	These caregivers may even eventually adopt the child. The child refers to these caregivers as mom and dad or aunt and uncle, or uses some other term of endearment.
Biological parents with their girlfriends or boyfriends	Girlfriends and boyfriends often are called mom or dad, even if they are not biological parents or stepparents by marriage. Some students have had a revolving door of moms and dads in their lives. Somewhere in this mix is often the ex-husband or ex-wife who also has custody of some sort.
Stepparents	Stepparents can have varying degrees of parental responsibilities, depending on the individual family dynamic. This works well when the biological parents and stepparents of both families get along. It can be problematic when they do not.
Biological mom and/or biological dad	These biological parents are sometimes married, but sometimes not. Sometimes it is a single-parent home.
Adoptive parents from foster care, international adoption, or domestic adoption	All adoptive parents should be considered *parents*, plain and simple. Adoption is part of their story, and can often explain some of the trauma the child has endured. An adoptive parent is not any less of a parent than a biological parent. If anything, these parents have worked harder to parent a child that has greater needs than an average child without any special needs.
Foster care parents	Licensed foster care parents have attended all of the trainings and have to abide by all of the state laws about caring for a child in foster care. They are also paid by the state to care for children.
Relative caregiver, fictive kin, or "suitable other" foster care parent	Fictive kin is a term used to refer to individuals who are unrelated by either birth or marriage to the child, but have an emotionally significant relationship, and have agreed to take a child into their homes. They have not received any training, their homes do not have to be held to the same standards of safety as a licensed foster care home, and they do not receive any payments from the state to care for the child placed in their home.

FIGURE 1.2   Typology of Today's Students

Type of Student	Description
Highly gifted, above grade level	Students whose test scores exceed a certain level as defined by the school, district, or state guidelines.
On-grade-level students	Students whose test scores are at or above proficiency.
Students with disabilities	About 13% of public school students have been evaluated and placed in special education programs. This includes students ages 3–21. These students may be served in self-contained classrooms or through pullout services with a resource teacher.
RTI students	Students receiving interventions and being monitored for their responses to those interventions.
English language learners	Educational models and programs of service vary according to the educational theory selected by the school (ESL, transitional bilingual education, dual language, etc.).
Included students	Students who have qualified for services in one of 13 categories of special education because their educational performance has been adversely affected. These students are included in the regular classroom and receive modifications in the educational program to include both curriculum and instructional methods. About 63% of students with disabilities spend at least 80% of their school day in general education classrooms.

Source: Information and statistics regarding special education have been adapted from Heasley (2018)

Reprinted from *How to Deal With Parents Who Are Angry, Troubled, Afraid, or Just Seem Crazy: Teachers' Guide* by Elaine K. McEwan-Adkins. Thousand Oaks, CA: Corwin, www.corwin.com. Reproduction authorized for educational use by educators, local school sites, and/or noncommercial or nonprofit entities that have purchased the book.

to help their children. Some of these parents are trying but don't have the necessary tools to help their children from hard places, and other parents are doing an incredible job of trying to support their children through their trauma. The other group of children that struggles are still living in traumatic family lives. They are currently in homes where parents are verbally abusive, neglectful, or struggling so much with their own issues that they aren't able to care properly and support their children, because they can barely take care of themselves.

FACET 3: A CONTINUUM OF TYPES OF SCHOOLS

The type of school (see Figure 1.3) in which you currently work can either help or hinder you when it comes to dealing with dysfunctional parents. In fact, the school culture in which you work is seldom added into the mix when teasing out the reasons for a growing number of angry parents. For example, in underperforming schools, the achievement of struggling students (who are constantly in need of extra support from their parents) is masked by the achievement of high-performing students. The community and staff members may perceive the school to be a good one, but it is not increasing the academic capacity of all students, and consequently there is a contingent of angry parents whose issues and complaints are often given short shrift by teachers.

FIGURE 1.3   A Typology of Schools

Type of School	Description
Highly effective	An equitable and excellent school that enables all of its students, regardless of their demographics or categorical labels, to achieve academic success.
Effective	An equitable and excellent school that enables at least 95% of its students, regardless of their demographics or categorical labels, to achieve academic success.
Good	A school that is moving steadily toward effectiveness but is not quite there yet. Many, if not all, of the traits usually found in a good school are present, but student achievement is not yet at 95%.
Transitional	A school that was once failing or underperforming but is now steadily improving. The transitional school is vulnerable to inalterable variables, such as the loss of a strong instructional leader or key teacher leaders, an unexpected influx of students due to boundary changes or natural disasters such as Hurricane Katrina, violence and death in the community or school, or the death, suicide, or serious illness of a student or faculty member.
Underperforming	A school where student achievement is acceptable to most observers, unless one considers the school's demographics. Educators in the school feel little accountability for the achievement of struggling students in their classrooms, and many of its teachers are underachieving along with their students. The achievement of high-performing students masks the low achievement of other students. The community may perceive this school to be a "good" school, but it is not increasing the academic capacity of all students.

Type of School	Description
Stuck	A school that is in an achievement "rut." The school is not declining, but neither is it improving. Test scores remain fairly stable year after year—not failing, but not great, given the demographics of the student body. Leadership is not focused on building academic capacity.
Low performing	A school in which the principal and teachers are good people who care for their students and work very hard. The educators in this school make periodic attempts to raise achievement, but their expectations are low, and their energies are largely focused on making themselves and their students feel good. School leaders are not committed to building academic capacity.
Dysfunctional	A school that has not been officially labeled as failing, but a toxic culture and absence of academic press have resulted in extraordinarily low student achievement.
Failing	A school that has failed to make its academic targets and has been placed under sanctions by the state or federal government.

Source: McEwan (2008)

Reprinted from *How to Deal With Parents Who Are Angry, Troubled, Afraid, or Just Seem Crazy: Teachers' Guide* by Elaine K. McEwan-Adkins. Thousand Oaks, CA: Corwin, www.corwin.com. Reproduction authorized for educational use by educators, local school sites, and/or noncommercial or nonprofit entities that have purchased the book.

When questioned about whether today's parents have become more difficult than they were in earlier decades, contributing educator Tresa Watson explained it this way:

I don't know that parents are more difficult to deal with now, but I do think there are more parents who struggle with knowing what to do with their children when issues are brought up, whether it be academic or behavioral. I believe there is less interaction between children and parents for numerous reasons from almost the moment of birth. Many parents work long hours and their relationships with off-spring aren't as strong as they were in the past. Children spend much more time on their own and with technology than with playmates, which inhibits their develop-ment of appropriate social-emotional skills. As each generation passes, I believe our societal trends have caused families to be less cohesive with fewer positive role models available. All of the moving parts of this facet of school life change the conversation teachers have with parents. In the past, most parent contact focused on academic concerns or serious behavioral issues. Now it seems that more parents need guidance and help with problem-solving for a wide range of issues with their children and they need it frequently. In fact, parents need our support and empathy as much as their children do.

FACET 4: THE THINGS TEACHERS DO THAT IRRITATE AND INFLAME PARENTS

Figure 1.4, The Things Teachers Do That Irritate and Inflame Parents, describes a range of teacher behaviors. Singly or in combinations, these behaviors can ignite an explosion that you will long remember.

FIGURE 1.4   The Things Teachers Do That Irritate and Inflame Parents

Type of Teacher Behavior	Description
Communication issues	Failure to communicate in a timely way is the number one reason why parents get angry. To avoid this problem, build communication networks and routines very early in the school year.
Procrastination	Telling parents that you will do something about a problem and then failing to do anything is a biggie that bugs parents. Promising to call a parent back and then misplacing the message is another "no no."
Stereotypes and biases	Putting labels on parents or assuming some character flaw because of their marital status, religious beliefs, sexual orientation, color, ethnicity, or socioeconomic status makes parents angry, and justifiably so. Whether these labels are unspoken or blurted out in a momentary slip of the tongue, your body language often speaks louder than words.
Defensiveness	Becoming defensive whenever a parent questions your actions or motives is a natural but highly unwise reaction. Your behavior will surely escalate what could have been a calm discussion into a heated exchange on both sides.
Overuse of educational jargon	Your inability to explain what you are doing and why in plain language that parents can understand gets them very upset. The use of jargon and acronyms is often pervasive in parent meetings for students in special programs or in meetings to decide where a student with special needs should be placed.
Dishonesty	Teachers don't tell outright lies very often, but when they do, usually to cover something clueless they did, the parent-teacher relationship can be irreparably damaged.

Type of Teacher Behavior	Description
Unwillingness to admit mistakes	All teachers have done their share of inadvisable things. After all, we are human. We are not the paragons of virtue we might pretend to be. Parents and even your administrator will usually forgive a mistake, bad judgment, or a momentary lapse of common sense. But what neither parents nor your supervisor can abide is an unwillingness on your part to admit the mistake and apologize.

Consider a scenario in which a set of biological parents with a rocky marriage are attending a meeting to hear the results of the special education team's evaluation of their child. They have brought a parent advocate to be their voice in the meeting. There are at least six other individuals around a long rectangular table: the classroom teacher, a school psychologist who assessed the student, a speech therapist who has participated in some RTI instruction, the principal, and the special education resource teacher. The silence in the room is awkward, and the educators are glancing at one another, obviously wondering who will chair the meeting. The first person to speak is the father, who is obviously growing more irritated at what seems to him to be a poorly organized meeting. In his business, someone would have greeted the parents and introduced all of the participants in the meeting. He is obviously going to reach his boiling point, and the meeting has not even started.

If you were observing this meeting to figure out the communication dynamics, you could check off multiple types of behavior that were slowly irritating and inflaming the father. The parent advocate may be the next meeting participant to feel some anger at the way her clients are being treated. This brief snapshot illustrates how easily teachers (and other educators) can do things that irritate and inflame parents.

Contributing educator Justin Gremba had a surprising answer when asked about what he wished he knew then (after an encounter with an angry parent) and what he knows now:

The answer may surprise you, but nothing. I truly believe that a lot of this job deals with hands-on experiences. Experienced teachers are extremely helpful, but living through these experiences is a necessary part of the job. What I wish is that every one of my colleagues would actually learn from their experiences and continue to improve how they deal with angry parents.

Avoid writing terse emails that contain "deficit" language that immediately upsets parents. Consider this example of a real email from a teacher to a parent: "Your child is struggling with understanding division. Your child did not complete the in-class assignment. Please make sure your child completes the catch-up assignment tonight." This sounds like a charging document for a court case rather than an email from a caring teacher. Unfortunately, the educator couldn't take the time to plug the child's name into the email template she was using. It sounds to the parent like the teacher is offloading her responsibility for explaining division in a way that her daughter can understand it to the parents, who may not have been briefed on the newest approach to teaching division. What if Emily has piano lessons after dinner? There is trouble brewing on the horizon. The entire family will be up until the wee hours deciphering the math assignment. The sound you are hearing in the background of this scenario is daughter Sarah having a meltdown: "My teacher doesn't like me. Do you think I'm still a good person because I can't do math?" This teacher has just lost the trust of both the parent and the child by suggesting that whenever she can't teach your child, you will have to take up the slack or pay for pricey math tutoring.

FACET 5: A VARIETY OF TYPES OF PARENTS

Figure 1.5, Typology of Parents, describes in great detail the variety of types of parents whose paths may well cross yours. Sometimes the type of school can dictate the type of parents you will encounter.

FIGURE 1.5 Typology of Parents

Type of Parent	Description
Entitled	These parents see the school system as another service they are "hiring" for their student, similar to the way they hire a cleaning staff at their home or how they pay for a club or a sport. As such, the relationship between school and parent becomes one of service provider and client rather than institution and participant. These successful parents are very used to having employees and organizations cater to their needs; throughout the day they may be in professional situations in which they are constantly telling people what to do, with the expectation that their needs will be met. That sort of worldview doesn't fade away when it comes to their child's schooling. (Adapted by permission from material contributed by Jillian D'Angelo)

Type of Parent	Description
Paragons of parenting	The most culturally relevant trophy or award that adults can present to verify their success in life is a successful accomplished child. Parents' self-esteem and self-worth now rest heavily on their child's "value" in society, and that value can be measured in various ways depending on what is a priority for the given parents. Some parents measure it with athletic dominance, some with academic prowess, still others with social status. As a result, it can become increasingly difficult, if not impossible, for parents to hear that there may be any flaw, problem, or abnormality with their child. Not only is this a blow to their image of who their child is, but it is a direct blow to the parents' own feelings of self-confidence and self-worth. Very few humans can absorb such personal attacks without some psychological protections. The easiest protections to adopt are denial and transference. And so, you often see parents who think their children can do no wrong, and who struggle to hear feedback from teachers. Rather than address problems their student might be having (either academic or behavioral) and give the support the student needs to feel success, the parents deny the problem exists and lash out at the teacher, blaming the problem on the teacher's decision making, education experience, or instructional expertise. It can't be my child that's wrong; it must be the teacher. (Adapted by permission from material contributed by Jillian D'Angelo)
Perfect all-purpose parent	These parents don't hover or hang around school. They likely have full-time jobs. However, they always show up for parent-teacher conferences and accept feedback and suggestions from teachers. They trust that if someone reports to them that their child has broken a rule, they will fully agree that consequences are necessary. They sign every form, contribute to every fund-raising drive, and show up at school board meetings to lobby for smaller class sizes.
Prone to anger when aroused by teachers	These parents *could* be perfect all-purpose parents, but they do have their limits. Life is stressful for them, their time is valuable, and they deserve to be treated with respect. They may be single parents, work two part-time jobs, and have at least one child with a learning difficulty. They are especially prone to anger when they experience a teacher's inappropriate behavior and there is no forthcoming apology.
Unprepared parents	These parents struggle with knowing what to do with their children when academic or behavioral issues are brought to their attention. Seemingly from the moment of birth, there is less interaction between these parents and their children. The reasons are numerous. Many parents work long hours, and relationships with their children aren't as strong as they were in the past. Children spend more time on their own and with technology than with playmates, which can inhibit their development of appropriate social-emotional skills. As each generation passes, our societal trends have caused extended families to be less cohesive, offering fewer

(Continued)

FIGURE 1.5   (Continued)

Type of Parent	Description
Unprepared parents (continued)	role models for children. This demographic impacts the conversations we have with parents. In earlier generations, parent-teacher contact focused primarily on academic concerns or serious behavioral issues. In contrast, these parents need guidance with problem solving for a wide range of issues with their children, and they often need it frequently. These parents need as much support as their children do. (Adapted by permission from material contributed by Joelle Wright)
Missing in action, uninvolved, uncommunicative	These parents are difficult if not impossible to engage in their child's learning and school experience. This attitude has a detrimental effect on both their student's academic growth and their behavior. If parents don't care about their child's education, this attitude rubs off on the student. The uncommunicative parent can be the most difficult to deal with, especially if the child involved is struggling academically or behaviorally. Look for ways to help that child be successful, but if you don't have the ability to communicate with the parent about what factors outside of school may be impacting the child, or ideas for how interventions might work or be received by the family, making gains that last from day to day is difficult. Missing-in-action parents may be homeless or living in poverty and have few options for getting to your school. They may be addicted to drugs or alcohol and may be too incapacitated or embarrassed to make it to school for a conference.
Disadvantaged	Disadvantaged families often appreciate the value of education and are supportive of teachers and all of the sacrifices they make. These parents may be struggling with poverty or immigration issues, and they are under the constant pressures of finding suitable housing. They will need a variety of support services, including free and reduced-price lunches, school breakfasts, and possibly translation. Although they are disadvantaged in many material ways, these parents have children who will work as hard as you expect them to work and achieve to levels you never thought possible.
History of educational trauma	Although these parents will not likely discuss their history with you, some have experienced deep-seated trauma from an earlier encounter with an ineffective teacher, a bully administrator, or a sexual pervert who has been abusive. This whole package of past traumas can explode on you in many ways, but trying to convince parents that you are different and you really do care will consume far more of your time than you likely have available.
Dysfunctional	These parents have a variety of mental illnesses: depression, bipolar disorder, personality disorders. These problems make it very difficult for them to work with educators, and as soon as you seem to get one problem solved, they pop in your door with three more.
Mentally ill, addicted	These parents need very special handling and as much professional assistance as you have available.

The effect of divorce rates is noted by contributing educator Andrew Lucas:

Another factor that makes today's parents more difficult to deal with is the higher frequency of divorce. This has a huge effect on the child, and the first place you see it is in the classroom. These days I'm more surprised to find that a struggling student is from a home where the parents are still together (though that could just be me glorifying the past). Over the past five years, in particular, we've seen some very messy divorces, where parents are fighting over the kids and trying to get the children to take sides. Small wonder these children can't focus in school.

Contributing educator Nancy Adamson shared this observation:

Twenty-five years ago, mothers stayed home or worked part-time so they were more involved with their children's education. The parents of today put most of the responsibility for their child's education on the teachers. When problems arise, parents find it more convenient to blame the teacher. As a result, parents who don't support what the school is trying to do are often completely oblivious to either the capabilities or problems of their children.

There is a one-liner that used to be heard in many classrooms on back-to-school nights: Teachers jokingly would say to the parents seated before them in too-small desks or unstable tables: "I won't believe what your kids tell me about you if you won't believe what your kids have to say about me." That tired wisecrack may be completely out of date today. Contributing educator Kathy Hoedeman relates a rather disturbing trend in her middle school:

There is a common feeling in my school, especially regarding behavior and discipline issues. Parents have become less willing to accept the views of educators regarding their children. Many faculty members have had the experience in which parents just cannot accept the fact that their child is in the wrong. The side of the child is taken over that of the adult teacher. Our middle school building is now full of video cameras and more than a few times our principal has had to refer to taped "proof" of behaviors in order to get parents to accept the fact that their children are guilty and must accept the consequences of their behaviors. Some teachers feel that this attitude on the part of parents has caused our administration to fail to pursue some issues with the seriousness they deserve simply because they don't want to deal with argumentative parents.

Contributing educator Robyn Ross finds the missing-in-action parents to be the most troublesome for her.

I will never understand the parents who choose to avoid me and direct every communication (no matter how large or small) to the principal. When parents effectively shut me out of the communication loop by responding to my phone messages, emails, and notes by ignoring me, I can't help but wonder what I did to deserve this shunning. No matter what avenues my principal or I have tried, they refuse to communicate with me as the classroom teacher. Parenting styles and interactions have run the gamut during my teaching career but in the past five years I have noticed a definite trend toward the uninvolved/uncommunicative parent. Granted, there are many factors that come into play, but it has become more and more difficult to engage parents in their child's learning and school experience. This has a detrimental effect on both a student's academic growth and their behavior. If parents don't care about their child's education, this attitude rubs off on the student. I find that the uncommunicative parent can be the most difficult to deal with, especially if the child involved is struggling academically or behaviorally. I am constantly looking for ways to help that child be successful, but if I don't have the ability to communicate with the parent about what factors outside of school may be impacting the child, or ideas for how interventions might work or be received by the family, making gains that last from day to day is difficult.

There are five chapters ahead with pages and pages of ways to deal productively with angry parents. Figure 1.6 contains a handy organizer to help you remember the big idea of this chapter: *Just when you think you have a handle on how best to deal with angry parents, two or three unexpected variables will make your task infinitely more challenging. Be prepared for anything.*

For example, here are just a few of the variables that can derail your attempts to soothe and calm an angry parent:

- Parents who are unprepared for the tasks you expect them to undertake with regard to supporting their students

- A school culture that is in transition from an influx of students who have experienced a weather trauma in another state

FIGURE 1.6   Quick Start Chart for Dealing With Angry Parents

The Root of the Anger	Things to Do	Things Not to Do	Exacerbating Variables
A situation that involves or concerns their children	Remain calm. Apologize if appropriate. Offer to hold another meeting. Offer to invite a specialist or someone who has answers for the parents' questions. This type of anger can often be resolved very easily if you keep your cool; don't become defensive; offer a quick apology even if you're not at fault for anything, and throw in a compliment about their child and an affirmation of their great parenting skills.	Don't interrupt. Don't become defensive. Don't argue. Don't raise your voice. Don't fidget. Don't furrow your brow. Don't squint your eyes. Don't cross your arms. Don't try to convince the parent that you can fix the problem.	A low-performing school that promises improvement but never delivers leaving parents with frustration. Teachers make promises and then never deliver on those pledges. The parents are in the middle of a messy divorce and are so busy fighting with each other that they take out their anger and rage at teachers. The dysfunctional school culture fails to support effective teachers, and the low expectations nearly always result in low student achievement.
A serious dysfunction in their life that is exacerbated by a problem or concern with their child	Remain calm. Employ active listening. Give the parents enough time to exhaust their ranting and raving. Remember that they have the problem, not you or the child.	Don't interrupt. Don't try to come up with a solution. Don't get restless or look at your watch.	Unprepared parents who are unable to follow through on any suggestions or help you offer. The school is in transition after an influx of students from another state who have undergone a weather trauma.

(Continued)

FIGURE 1.6   (Continued)

The Root of the Anger	Things to Do	Things Not to Do	Exacerbating Variables
Genuine mental health issues that you are likely not ever going to understand or ameliorate.	Invite a specialist or an administrator to sit in on the meeting.	Don't overwhelm the parent with more than two other participants. Don't give the parent the feeling that you are ganging up on him or her.	The school is stuck, and there are few resources to support struggling students and novice teachers.
Past experience with another educator, another school, or their own failure at some point in school.	Empathy is your best strategy in this situation. Who wouldn't empathize with a horrendous school experience that has left someone with trauma, illiteracy, and low self-worth? Listen to the story the parent is telling. It may inform.	Don't interrupt while this parent is telling his or her story. If you must give advice, make it wordless.	Fearful parents who are convinced that their child will experience the same school failure that has traumatized them.

- Fearful parents who are convinced that their children won't have the opportunities they need to be successful

- A "stuck" school that covers up the poor performance of a struggling school with a majority of higher-achieving students

- Lack of trust between parents and teacher

Use Figure 1.6 to review what to do and what not to do when confronted with an angry parent. You may not achieve a perfect score the first time around, but hopefully your recognition and understanding of the many exacerbating variables will increase your empathy, care, and concern for the parents and students with whom you work.

SUMMING UP AND LOOKING AHEAD

The challenges in education (whether in public or private settings) today are enormous, and the need for teachers who have character, communication skills, and empathy has never been greater. More parents than ever are angry, troubled, afraid, or even crazy. In the face of this onslaught, you must be calm, thoughtful, caring, intelligent, articulate, direct, and honest. In a nutshell, you've got to walk on water *and* leap tall buildings in a single bound.

> Just when you think you have a handle on how best to deal with angry parents, two or three unexpected variables will make your task infinitely more challenging. Be prepared for anything.

If you feel unprepared to handle the challenges, don't be alarmed. Help is just ahead. Chapter 2 presents more than two dozen actions you can take at the beginning of the school year to become a proactive teacher—an educator who foresees where the problems and roadblocks may lie and develops routines, procedures, and policies to forestall disaster and engage proactively with parents.

CHAPTER 2

PROACTIVE WAYS TO GET AND KEEP PARENTS ON YOUR SIDE

There is no substitute for having a detailed plan as you head into
any high-stakes, stressful, and complex endeavor, whether it is the first 3 weeks
of a school year [or a meeting with a dysfunctional parent].

—Elaine K. McEwan (2006, p. 3)

The most effective way to deal with all parents is proactively. Don't wait for the storm clouds to gather. Get out ahead of parent problems by implementing some of the more than two dozen tips found just ahead. There are too many to implement all at once. But, if you choose one or two of the tips and consistently follow through with them from the beginning of the school year to the end, your hard work will pay off in positive and productive parent relationships.

1. Do all you can to establish a cooperative relationship with parents.

Students are more successful in school when you work cooperatively with their parents.

Parents will be more supportive and willing to give you the benefit of the doubt, even in stress-filled and emotional encounters, when you have established a history of working together from your very first encounter with them. Contributing educator Tresa Watson recommends,

> When dealing with families that you suspect might be a bit dysfunctional, always reach out from the perspective of seeking their support, affirming that they are the experts and advocates for their children, even when it sometimes doesn't seem they are. Parents will be more supportive and willing to give you the benefit of the doubt, even in stress-filled and emotional encounters, when you have established a history of working together from your very first encounter with them.

2. Cultivate administrative support.

If you are concerned that a certain parent may pose a problem to you, talk to your administrator as soon as possible to make sure you are clear on the relevant school/district policy. You and your principal should present a united front. Potentially difficult parents take their concerns to the principal rather quickly, so make sure that whatever you told the parent will be confirmed by the principal. There is nothing more demoralizing than being undermined by your supervisor. (Adapted by permission from material contributed by Jillian D'Angelo)

3. Drop a postcard in the mail to your students during the first three weeks of school.

Before the school year begins, address a postcard to each student. You can buy postcards in packs at teacher supply stores. As the school year begins, look for students doing something exemplary. The minute you spot a noteworthy action, take that student's preaddressed card from the pile, write the note, and mail it immediately to the student at home. For example, you might write, "I noticed you cleaned up the book corner without being asked to do so. Thank you for taking the time to invest in our classroom." Parents will see the postcard and immediately feel (a) that you recognize the value of their child and (b) that you care. When they have that first impression of you, future meetings are more likely to be characterized by trust. The added benefit is that kids love getting their own mail. Try to get all students' cards sent by the third week of school.

To set the stage and prime the pump for students on the first day of school, post classroom jobs with a short description of what each job entails. When you introduce the various jobs, explain to students that even if it is not their job that week, if they see something that needs to be done, they are expected to complete that task. The postcards are not just for reinforcing housekeeping chores. They can also be used to encourage particularly shy students to participate. For example, "Dear Julie, when you shared that story about your family vacation in class, all of the students were able to see the connection to the book we are reading. I can't wait to hear more of the wonderful things you have to say this school year."

4. Proactively seek counsel and support from your principal and colleagues as well as the specialized personnel in your school or district, such as the psychologist, a counselor, or a behavior management specialist.

Don't ever think you need to handle a problem all by yourself, or subscribe to the mistaken notion that you should know all the answers. The wisdom of others can help relieve the burden of dealing with a particularly difficult parent on your own. It really does "take a village."

5. If at first you stumble a bit, pick yourself up and try again.

Although you may be reluctant to reach out to parents after a less than successful first meeting, do not hesitate to do so. After a week or two the parents may have calmed down and will appreciate that you made the first move.

6. Give a rapid but thoughtful response to what you think is a communique from a "blow everything out of proportion" parent.

Dealing with parents in general can be tricky, but dealing with difficult parents can be like walking through a mine field. I find that being as proactive with positive communication as possible is helpful with "blow everything out of proportion" parents, since it often keeps them from going there. Rapid but thoughtful responses (whether via phone or email), and efforts to work with the parent to join your team with the best interest of the child in mind, are helpful tools. (Adapted by permission from material contributed by Robyn Ross)

7. Start early and be persistent.

Establish contact with parents early in the school year. For example, send a letter to parents before school starts. Welcome them and their child to your "classroom community." Introduce yourself by including a few details about yourself (e.g., you have two rescue dogs, or you play in a weekend soccer league, or your favorite food is fried chicken), and tell them how eager you are to meet them at the Back-to-School open house. Make sure you have extra letters prepared to give to families who register after the preregistration process. Then have a file in which you place important memos and explanations for families who may move in during the school year.

8. Be prepared with data.

Be sure to have concrete data to rely on when parents' perception of their child's performance is very different from yours. Data can be the difference between a "my way"/ "no, my way" discussion and a productive meeting that benefits the student in the future. It is better to inundate parents with information than to surprise them with concerns halfway through the year. Make sure to regularly update the class website and newsletter, call or email parents of more difficult students to check in, and set up meetings with parents when you have concerns in advance of parent-teacher conferences. A parent should never hear a serious concern for the first time at a conference or read about it on a report card. These official forms of communication are more formal and are often seen as "high-stakes" by parents. Hearing bad news when weeks of the school year have already gone by will more likely elicit backlash and defensive behavior. (Adapted by permission from material contributed by Jillian D'Angelo)

9. Build rapport.

The teacher who has a close and meaningful connection with every student is more likely to have a very successful year. Teacher contributor Justin Gremba explains rapport in this way:

> As a parent, when I attend a school function for my kids, I only care about one thing. That "thing" is the well-being of my child. I am always impressed by a teacher who says or does something that indicates that the teacher has developed rapport and is focused on the well-being of my child. As a teacher I make it my number one priority to build rapport and make connections with my own students. I make it a point to find out what they like to do, what their favorite games or movies are, and what goes on in their lives.

10. On your mark, get set, go.

This is a strategy contributing educator Jillian D'Angelo adapted from the book *Teach Like a Champion 2.0* (Lemov, 2014). She teaches it to her students at the beginning of the school year, and it becomes an everyday routine. The concept is that there is a set expectation for what a student's desk and/or locker looks like before class starts (pencil out and sharpened, homework turned in, notebook open to new page, etc.). In a self-contained classroom, you can either do this at the beginning of each new subject, or use it like I did at the beginning and end of the day. In the classroom I had pictures and a list of descriptions of not only what the students' individual work spaces needed to look like, but what the whole classroom needed to look like before class could start, and again before students could leave at the end of the day. (The descriptions included things like classroom library in order, construction paper organized and put away, coats hanging neatly in lockers, etc.) Practice this often enough, and the only cue the students need is "You need to be on your mark in five minutes," or "I see three students who need to be on their mark," and the students know to check the list and make sure they are completely ready for the day. Having the list and pictures posted for reference (or you could have it taped to each student's desk) allows them to independently take responsibility for maintenance of the room.

11. Implement an open-door policy.

Implement an open-door policy when it comes to parents volunteering or visiting your classroom. Often just knowing they are welcome at any time will put parents at ease and prevent "hovering" that may become an issue for student and teacher. Be sure to clear this policy with your principal and school safety officer (if you have one). Also, make clear to parents that your school has firm rules about first going to the office to sign in and receive a visitor's badge. Parents who refuse to follow those simple rules will lose their visitation privileges.

12. Check my spelling and grammar, please.

Ask a trusted colleague or the office secretary (if the weekly memos are always perfect) to proofread a communication before sending it out. In addition to checking for inadvertent spelling and grammar errors, a pair of more experienced eyes can alert you to some policy or procedure that clashes with the content of your email.

13. Invite students to be part of your parent-teacher conferences.

When you invite students to be a part of your first parent-teacher conference, you will accomplish two things. Parents will hopefully be on their best behavior in the presence of their child. And, if there are academic or behavioral issues that need to be resolved, all of the key players in solving the problem will be sitting around the table. If you do need to discuss anything of a private nature, you can always ask the student to step out of the room and wait in the hallway.

14. Offer parents a menu of communication options.

In today's world you have multiple options to offer parents concerning how they want to receive information from you: via email, a post on social media, a text message, or a paper copy of some critically important policy that needs a signature from the parent. Consider the purpose of the communication you will be sending: general information sent to every parent, information that is private and related to a specific school problem, or a special alert bulletin to every parent concerning a classroomwide issue, like a serious outbreak of head lice or the fact that the boiler that heats your classroom will be down for repairs tomorrow, and if your child gets chilled very easily, send extra clothes or pile on the long underwear.

15. Send home a parent survey at the beginning of the school year.

Give parents an opportunity to enumerate their child's strengths as well as share any pertinent behavioral or academic areas that are of concern. Ask questions about activities their children like to play or equipment they like to use in recreation, how they like to play, and what extracurricular activities or sports they may engage in outside of school.

16. Develop specific agendas for various types of parent meetings.

There are three possible types of parent meetings you will no doubt hold: (1) regularly scheduled parent-teacher conferences, (2) a meeting with parents that you have requested to discuss specific issues and problems you are having with the student, and (3) a meeting with you that the parents have requested.

1. The first type of meeting is the regularly scheduled parent conference usually held in the fall and spring of the school year. You are expected and required to meet with

parents to report a student's progress during the first quarter of the school year. There may be a standardized agenda that you are expected to follow in the conference as well as a form to complete to take notes about any critical information exchanged or decisions made about a new direction for the student.

2. The second type of meeting is one that you have requested. You want to talk with parents about an academic or behavioral concern that needs a face-to-face discussion. Sending emails about sensitive concerns can cause parents to worry needlessly or spiral into an angry tirade.

3. The third type of meeting is one that the parents have requested. Prior to the meeting, attempt to find out the purpose of the meeting. If the parent has not been forthcoming about the purpose of the meeting, do a little detective work. Speak with the previous year's teacher to see if there were any issues or hot buttons that popped up during the year. Ask your administrator if he or she knows or has been contacted by the parents and has suggested they ask for a meeting with you. If you don't know what the reason is, be prepared to have some nice things to say about their child. And then be ready to listen.

17. Give advance warning.

Give parents ample warning if you plan to make any changes in your classroom procedures, schedules, or grading requirements. For those parents who didn't have a chance to read the first memo you sent, consider giving parents several warnings. If available, print the notice on neon paper that will get their attention. If you have children of your own, you *do* understand the chaos that can ensue at home when you find out that you fell asleep reading your email, or threw away the important notice in the trash. Avoid relying completely on students delivering the notice.

18. Respect parents' schedules.
Start and end meetings on time.

Rehearse your agenda before the first parent-teacher conferences. In your rehearsal, hit the main idea of each agenda point, and keep on schedule. There is nothing more frustrating to parents on their lunch break than to have the previously "scheduled" parent-teacher conference run well over the allotted time. If you sense that the currently scheduled parents are talking as though they have the whole day free for this conference and intend to take it, politely remind them that you have parents waiting in the hall. Suggest that they schedule another appointment to discuss a problem that has nothing to do with discussing the report card.

19. Recognize the special needs of single-parent families.

Be willing to set aside your traditional notions of a "good" family to benefit children who are being raised in more "contemporary" families. Provide child care for social events and parent-teacher conferences so that single parents can more easily attend.

20. Breaking up is hard to do.

Accommodating the needs of divorced parents often means going out of your way to provide dual report cards and separate parent-teacher conferences, but the payback in good will and support for a child already torn between mom and dad is worth it. Some districts are even willing to ease residency rules while families are in transition. That, of course, is a matter of policy.

21. Be sensitive to the cultural nuances in the families in your community.

Understanding the cultural contexts of students and families is especially important for building strong teacher-family bonds. Be sensitive to nonverbal communication cues, such as eye contact, personal space, and personal touch. Enlist the help of community and religious leaders to build bridges with the cultural or ethnic minorities in your classroom.

22. What's in a name?

Learn as many students' and parents' names as you can. Practice pronouncing them correctly as preferred by the student and the parents. Consult individuals on your staff that speak the language to help you. If you need reminders about the pronunciations, include a phonetic pronunciation guide in your list. Put name tags on tables and desks, so you can immediately start associating students' names and faces. After you've learned all of your students' names, learn something unique about each one. I have learned from doing countless presentations that there is no accounting for the unique names that mothers (or others) have conferred upon their children. Clearly some parents have completely broken through the conventions of grammar and spelling. However, honor those names and spellings. Learn to say and spell them the way the child and parents prefer, and don't stumble over that pronunciation every time you call on this child in your class. That qualifies as an insult every time you do it.

23. Say something nice.

Of course, you will be primed and ready to offer affirmations and compliments at the beginning of each regularly scheduled parent conference. However, also be prepared to offer the same kind of feedback when you run into a parent at the deli or coffee shop. Don't duck into the next aisle when you see parents at the grocery store. Use this encounter to build rapport and deposit a little cash in the "Relationship Trust and Savings Bank." Whenever you meet with a parent, hand out a compliment or two. Nothing will bring a smile and a glow to parents' faces faster than good news about their child.

24. Honor extended families.

Designate days on your calendar for grandparents' day or science fair displays, or use any other opportunity to bring extended family members into your classroom. Take care to choose these dates at the beginning of the year so that parents and extended family members can plan. Some people will need to request a personal day at the place of employment. Some grandparents (the fortunate ones) will have to book expensive plane reservations and need time to save for that expenditure. It's better not to plan such a day at all than to suddenly get a brainstorm two weeks before and blindside parents.

25. Put out the welcome mat.

Make your classroom an inviting place to visit. Let parents know that there will always be chairs available just inside the door. Display student artwork and other class projects in the hallway outside your door, and try to communicate the emphasis on learning that is present in your classroom.

26. Have a classroom open house.

In addition to schoolwide social events and informal gatherings, plan regular open-house events in your classroom to communicate important information about curriculum and to show off student work. Science fairs, art shows, young authors' conferences, and musical concerts give students an opportunity to shine. These events that do not require a sit-down meeting with the teacher—and will feature some art work, poetry, or science experiment—may be just the incentive a reluctant and missing-in-action parent might need to show up in your classroom.

27. What do your students need to know and be able to do?

What do you expect your students to know and be able to do when they exit your grade level? How well have you communicated that information to parents? Consider publishing a booklet that sets forth the expectations for your grade level or course.

28. Explain your behavioral expectations during your Back-to-School night.

In addition to sending home a paper copy of your behavioral expectations for parents to sign and return, consider sharing and explaining these expectations at your Back-to-School night. Contributing educator Susan Biltucci has two general rules in her fifth-grade classroom: *Respect yourself, others, and property,* and *Take responsibility for your choices and actions.* The terms *respect* and *responsibility* are big concepts, and many parents need more than just two words. In her plan, she spells out what each of those concepts entails, but she gives parents an opportunity to ask questions about her plan and how it works.

29. The dog ate it.

Install a homework hotline where students and parents can verify homework assignments. The same system can also accommodate absentee calls and include a calendar of upcoming events.

30. What kind of work do you do?

Invite parents to your classrooms to talk about their careers. Encourage them to bring along several items they use in their work and to come in their work clothing. Another event that will bring parents (and other relatives) to school is the opportunity to read their favorite story aloud in your classroom.

31. Ask a witness to come to any meetings you have scheduled with an angry or potentially explosive parent.

Ask your principal, counselor, SPED teacher, or any other person with a positive connection to the child to join you at your meeting. This is good idea for multiple reasons:

1. You will have a witness in the event the parent makes a wrongful accusation about something you say or neglect to say.

2. You have support to back you up and affirm to the parent why your decision or action plan was a good choice.

3. The presence of another person in the meeting might give parents reason to pause and collect their thoughts. They will be less likely to unload their pent-up emotions on you, if they realize there will be another person to listen to them.

4. Any individuals you have invited to the meeting can likely be more objective and help you to de-escalate the situation while not being emotionally involved. (Adapted by permission from material contributed by Joelle Wright)

32. Refer to parents as partners and experts.

Consistently refer to parents as "partners" and "experts" when it comes to helping their child. Don't do this to stroke their egos; do it because it's the truth. Parents know their child better than anyone else, and using this language sends a message that they have every right to engage in the educational process of their child. Some parents find the current educational system foreign and intimidating, so they lash out. Reaching out to them with an offering of partnership can often bring them around to your team. (Adapted by permission from material contributed by Andrew Lucas)

SUMMING UP AND LOOKING AHEAD

Hopefully, you have come upon a few proactive strategies you can incorporate into the routines, procedures, and daily life of your classroom and interactions with parents. Be forewarned that there will always be parents that need more specific help than that afforded by this chapter. Chapter 3 expands the universe of ways you can respond to angry and dysfunctional parents.

CHAPTER 3

DEFUSING AND DISARMING OUT-OF-CONTROL PARENTS

If you can keep your head when all about you

Are losing theirs and blaming it on you

—Rudyard Kipling (1936)

I f you are able to skillfully defuse the negative emotions of angry, troubled, fearful, and sometimes completely distraught parents, you will have passed your first on-the-job assessment with flying colors. In fact, your effectiveness as a teacher could well depend on your ability to "keep your head when all about you are losing theirs" (Kipling, 1936). Chapter 1 provided an overview of the universe of angry parents. If you were at all nervous about interacting with parents prior to reading it, you might jump to the conclusion that there is an epidemic of angry parents lying in wait to sabotage the first parent-teacher conference of your career. Relax. That is definitely not the case. However, you must remember that all parents who care deeply about their children are capable of becoming angry if they perceive their children are being treated unfairly, or jump to an erroneous conclusion based on misinformation or a report their child has given them. Perfectly logical parents can become illogical, and perfectly polite parents can say and do things that are definitely inappropriate. They are as human as you are.

WHAT IS ANGER?

The title of this book names four categories of parents that you might encounter: angry, troubled, afraid, or just seem crazy. As I have revisited these four categories in writing this book especially for teachers and simultaneously reviewed the anecdotes shared by the contributing educators, I have begun to conclude that most of the upset and distress of parents in all of the categories is rooted in anger.

You can no doubt think of at least one parent in your career who personifies the concept of *anger* for you. But consider the following definition of anger as a more productive one to help you understand and deal with angry parents: "Anger is an experience that occurs when a goal, value, or expectation that [parents] have chosen has been blocked or when [their] sense of personal worth is threatened" (Taylor & Wilson, 1997, p. 71). Anger can be aroused by both real *and* supposed wrongs. Parents with irrational and unfounded anger are convinced that everyone in the school or district is out to get them; they are *paranoid*, and you will never convince them that their anger is irrational.

The truth is that all parents can be angry parents when it comes to their children. The key to getting along with them is being able to recognize that most of the time, when parents get mad, it's because somebody has interfered with their hopes and dreams for their child. They have lost their grip on reality. Of course they will be angry when you tell them the truth about their child.

Recall Figure 1.6, Quick Start Chart for Dealing With Angry Parents, introduced in Chapter 1. The chart will give you the basics, but the remainder of this chapter contains dozens of strategies with more detailed descriptions. If you need a quick reminder, tape a photocopy of the chart into your plan book.

Real anger is an extraordinarily complex emotion that can signal displeasure, hurt, shame, pain, indignation, resentment, exasperation, or annoyance, all of which may range from mild to extreme. It's easy to confuse the emotional and physiological responses of anger with the ways in which parents (and their children) express their anger. Anger can manifest itself in aggressive behaviors like criticizing, yelling, teasing, ridiculing, or scolding; in physical responses such as hitting or hurting others; and in more passive ways like silence, withdrawal, or hostile body language (Taylor & Wilson, 1997, pp. 53–54). Cruel anger that is aggressive or passive-aggressive is different from a more neutral anger that is assertive in nature and seeks to express itself in constructive ways.

Parents can exhibit two types of anger: (1) a reflexive emotional response that occurs when parents feel that they or their child are being threatened, and (2) an inappropriate and socially unacceptable *acting out* of their anger, for example, throwing a tantrum or throwing a punch. The emotions of anger cannot be suppressed. The acting out of anger with cruel speech or violent actions (i.e., aggression), or with passive-aggressive responses like the silent treatment or sarcasm, are learned responses that can be unlearned or replaced with more appropriate and productive responses.

HOW TO DEAL WITH ANGRY PARENTS

There are dozens of individual strategies and tools that can be employed to deal with angry parents, but they work most effectively when you are a person of character. I submit character is the antidote to anger. Anger can be a poison that paralyzes relationships, nurtures mistrust, and suppresses and destroys the emotional immune system.

The Antidote to Anger: Good Character

One of the most powerful tools you have for nurturing cordial and productive relationships with parents is your own personal character. Stephen Covey (1998) believes that character is foundational to

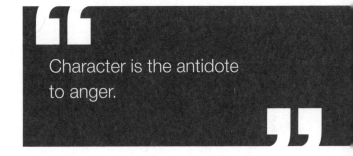

Character is the antidote to anger.

all that we aspire to be and do as educators: "Primary greatness is character" (p. 102). As a teacher you serve as a critical role model for both your students and their parents.

In 2002, I surveyed hundreds of parents, principals, teachers, and students, asking them to enumerate and prioritize the traits they considered essential in an effective teacher. I summarized the results in *10 Traits of Highly Effective Teachers* as follows: "The highly effective teacher is positive and real, demonstrating the qualities of respect, caring, empathy, and fairness in his/her communications and relationships with students, parents, and colleagues" (McEwan, 2002, p. 29).

None of us is perfect, but our very human failings and those of distraught parents should never be an excuse for not striving to teach and model the traits of honesty, dependability, perseverance, self-control, orderliness, and patience. The character of your students often depends on your consistent attention to building your own character in your everyday behavior in the classroom. You may be the most important, or in some cases, the only character-builder in their lives. Remember that what you demand from your students must also be modeled by you for their parents. If you preach punctuality, make sure you're on time for parent meetings. If you encourage students to be orderly, make sure that your classroom looks reasonably tidy in time for a conference. If you expect students to be friendly (knowing, liking, and accepting other people just the way they are), then you must be friendly to their parents. Hamachek (1999) summarizes teachers with character in this way:

> All in all, the evidence seems quite clear when it comes to describing good or effective teachers on the basis of personal characteristics; effective teachers appear to be those who are, shall we say, "human" in the fullest sense of the word. They have a sense of humor, are fair, empathetic, more democratic than autocratic, and apparently can relate easily and naturally to students on either a one-to-one or group basis. (p. 212)

Dealing effectively with angry parents is very difficult if you are not someone who at the very least aspires to be an individual of high character. No one is a paragon of perfection when it comes to character, and "to understand our encounters with difficult people, we eventually need to accept the fact that we are them" (Rosen, 1998, p. 20), but then, we must daily aspire to be individuals of character to whom parents and students can look to for leadership. With character traits like trustworthiness, integrity, authenticity, and respect on your side, you will have "money in the Relationship Trust and Savings Bank" when it comes to dealing with unhappy parents.

Ways to Be as a Teacher of Good Character

Regrettably, you cannot purchase character traits on the internet or earn credits for them by reading books by Stephen Covey. Your character is the result of your beliefs, which express themselves in your behaviors and habits over time. The very good news is that you can always grow and develop positive character traits. To be a person of good, high-quality character, you must have your priorities aligned. They may not always stay perfectly aligned and may sometimes need what my father used to call "an attitude adjustment." Parents know teachers of good character when they see them. Those are the teachers they still remember from when they were in school. Today, they are the teachers they want for their children. There are five ways to be a person of good character: (1) be trustworthy, (2) be honest, (3) be authentic, (4) be respectful, and (5) be forgiving.

Be Trustworthy

Contributing educator Kim Baer has *her* priorities aligned:

> At the beginning of the school year, I stress to parents the need for us to trust each other. I endeavor to communicate to them that our classroom procedures and policies have been developed with the best interests of their child at heart. Once I have their trust they will stop feeling the need to question everything that goes on in my classroom.

The tricky tightrope is this: You can't *make* parents trust you. They either do or they don't, based on your behavior, your reputation, or experiences they've had with someone in the same position as yours. Some parents may reserve judgment until they've seen you in action themselves, others will take the word of a friend or neighbor (the grapevine is alive and well), and still others will make up their minds about you immediately, based on nothing more than a gut feeling. Building trust among parents is one of the most important tasks you will undertake as a teacher. Trust is the glue that holds relationships together through tough times. When parents trust you, they will give you the benefit of the doubt. They will approach you with an attitude of respect that says, "Even though I'm upset with you personally or have questions about the ways things are done in your classroom, I know that you're an intelligent, caring person who will try to understand where I'm coming from."

Be Honest

Integrity, the second important trait of character that gives you money in the problem-solving bank, consists of far more than just telling the truth. Integrity speaks of a unity and consistency of personal behavior that withstands the scrutiny and invites the confidence of parents. Educators of integrity are predictable, because they make decisions based on a coherent set of values. They know what they stand for and can articulate their beliefs with eloquence. If you handle problems based on the three Ps (politics, pressure, and power), you will soon have a reputation as someone who "blows in the wind," an educator who can be bullied and bought. With that kind of reputation, you can expect more than your fair share of parental problems.

Be Authentic

Authenticity means giving the same kind of attention and respect to everyone regardless of who they are, where they live, what they look like, or how they act. Autry (2001) says, "Be the same person in every circumstance. Hold to the same values in whatever role you have" (p. 10). Authentic teachers are consistent, predictable, and utterly transparent. They know who they are, and so do the parents whose children are in their classrooms.

> Integrity speaks of a unity and consistency of personal behavior that withstands the scrutiny and invites the confidence of parents.

Be Respectful

One doesn't usually think immediately of respect (i.e., consideration, courtesy, and attention) as a correlate of successful schools comparable to effective instruction, standards for learning, and instructional leadership. However, in their review of research on effective educators, Persell and Cookson (1982) found "a recurrent characteristic of successful schools concerns the amount of respect shown to all participants" (p. 23). Who better to model and teach respect for students than you, the classroom teacher.

Be Forgiving

You may think of forgiveness as a religious concept, and indeed, "forgiving one who has harmed you liberates you from the emotional prison you have created for yourself . . . [and] is a deeply spiritual act" (Rosen, 1998, p. 255), but forgiveness is also an essential way of being if you intend to remain in education for any length of time. You may think of forgiveness as something you do for someone else, but in reality, it is something you do for yourself. To retain the slings and darts of angry parents in your psyche is a sure way to lose the vision of why you became a teacher in the first place.

Actions to Take in Response to Angry Parents

Those who know don't talk.

Those who talk don't know.

Close your mouth,

Block off your senses,

Blunt your sharpness,

Untie your knots,

Soften your glare,

Settle your dust. (Lao-Tzu, 6th c. BCE/1988, p. 56)

The ancient wisdom of Lao-Tzu sums up the essence of being responsive. When in the initial stage of meeting with an angry parent, you will not ask questions or gather information; that comes later during the exploratory stage. Neither will you set goals, attempt to solve the problem, or tell parents what actions you will take. Save "leaping tall buildings in a single bound" for later. The responsive stage is all about "closing your mouth, untying your knots, and softening your glare." As Lao-Tzu advises, "Settle your dust" (in a chair pulled alongside a parent) and "close your mouth."

Defusing distressed parents often requires a measure of on-the-spot decision making. However, the more systematic your approach to handling parental concerns can become, the more likely you will feel confident no matter what or who comes walking through your classroom door. There are numerous strategies you can routinely use that will help you deal effectively with parents who are upset or even out of control, most of them quite commonsensical. Don't make the mistake of thinking, however, that just because these behaviors sound simple and are the obvious things to do, they will be easy to employ in the face of unexpected behavior from a parent. Integrating these strategies into your working life will take time, discipline, and a measure of maturity. You will stumble and fail occasionally. Many of these strategies are not behaviors most of us adopt naturally. They demand that you wrestle with your personal values and learn to manage your own emotions. Once you have these strategies firmly established in your own repertoire, you will find many problems solving themselves before your very eyes. These strategies fall into three categories: (1) responsive, (2) exploratory, and (3) action. (The terms *exploratory* and *action* are adapted from Kottler & McEwan, 1999). We will discuss the responsive strategies in this chapter and tackle the exploratory and action strategies in Chapter 4.

As you consider how best to integrate these three types of strategies into your personal communication style, remember that disarming hostile and frustrated parents is an art, not a science. In the beginning, choose a single strategy that you find difficult to use automatically and practice it with everyone you talk to. For me personally, listening intently without becoming distracted or losing focus was my first goal. You may have to work on being less defensive or monitoring your body language so that it doesn't exacerbate an already explosive situation.

A rule of thumb when working with angry parents is to utilize the strategies in a somewhat chronological fashion: (1) respond, (2) explore, and (3) act. However, every individual or parental unit is different. With some parents, the process may only take one meeting; with others, it may take months (or even years). That is the art of working with difficult parents—knowing, as the country western song goes, "when to hold and when to fold."

Assume There Are Problems

If parents make an appointment to meet with you, assume they have some kind of problem to discuss. So, don't immediately take over the conversation in such a way that they feel powerless to interrupt or change the subject. Rather, send the message that you are eager to have them share their concerns and give them "permission" to bring up a problem.

Welcome and Accept

Shake hands and welcome parents into your classroom. Even the most hostile parents will usually warm up a little bit to a personal greeting and a welcoming touch, if appropriate. Sit eye to eye and knee to knee. This practice is a key principle of group dynamics. It means that people need proximity to one another to connect. When people are seated too far away from one another, the space between them inhibits communication. Don't sit behind your desk when meeting with parents. Sit side by side at a round table that could include other participants if needed. Provide comfortable chairs and offer coffee, water, or a soft drink (if available) to put parents at ease.

Say Something Nice

Share a compliment about their child with the parents. If possible, do your homework before the meeting. Look at the student's cumulative folder and consult with specialists to determine any unique talents. Does this student have physical gifts that make him a standout in physical education? Is the child staying after school in the library learning programming? Dig a little and find out where a child shines, and make sure you share that with the parents. One genuine compliment will help to set a positive tone for the conference. Remember what your mother always said, "If you can't say something nice about somebody, don't say anything at all." So, before you do anything else, write out a compliment for every student in your classroom. Pull it out for a conference or mail a handwritten note to the parents. They will never forget that note and likely put it in a special place for safekeeping. Parents crave positive and affirming statements about their children.

Self-Neutralize

Sandra Crowe (1999) suggests that the first thing you do when confronted with difficult people is to self-neutralize. Repeat to yourself, "This isn't personal. It's not about me" (p. 121). And, most of the time it isn't about you. It's about teachers from the past, curricula, discipline procedures, and the baggage of emotional and physical stress that parents are dragging along with them wherever they go. When it isn't about "real" problems, it's usually about the parents' inability to accept the notion that someone else is in charge of their most precious possessions, their children.

Remaining neutral does not mean you lack empathy or have a dispassionate attitude toward parents who are distressed. It means that you should not feel responsible or take ownership of an angry parent's feelings and behavior. If parents are angry, upset, and troubled, it's not your fault. (Of course, if you really have blown it, by all means apologize and move on.) Do all you can do to defuse their anger, but then relax and sleep soundly. Don't let parents' anxiety, frustration, and hostility consume your energies and demoralize your own emotional state.

Attend

Being attentive to parents who are distressed is essential. Attending means giving people your undivided interest. It means using your body, your face, and especially your eyes to say, "Nothing exists right now for me except you. Every ounce of my energy and being is focused on you."

This kind of intense concentration calls for structuring one-on-one time with parents in an atmosphere that is free from interruptions. Clear away clutter. Remove anything that might interfere with your focus. Turn off the telephones and shut the door.

Angry parents, in particular, are often so used to being devalued by others that attending behaviors instantly tell them something is different about this interaction: "Here is a person who seems to care about me and what I have to say." But all adults in today's fast-track world will find having the full attention of an "important" person like their child's teacher a somewhat rare and enormously affirming experience.

Control Your Body Language

Communication consultant Marjorie Brody (2004) warns that your body language can often communicate how stressed you feel to those with whom you are speaking. Here are some tips to make sure that you appear relaxed and in control. The message you may be sending with your inappropriate nonverbal language is shown in parentheses.

- Don't stand with your hands on your hips (condescending and arrogant)
- Don't cross your arms (closed-minded and stubborn)
- Don't tap your fingers or other objects (impatient)
- Don't avoid eye contact (terrified)
- Don't stare intently (arrogant and intimidating)
- Don't droop your face, wrinkle your brow, or turn down your mouth in a frown (distressed, unhappy, or bored)
- Don't fidget in your chair (nervous, impatient, or disinterested)

Soften Your Speech

The tone and quality of your voice are just as important as the words you speak. If you are hurried, hostile, defensive, or distracted, your voice will give you away immediately, and parents will judge you to be insincere, even if you are saying all the right things. A soft answer means that you don't contradict, correct, condescend, or disagree with parents who are already infuriated, even if they are misinformed. Don't be impatient or act harried.

Convey serenity with body language that is calm and receptive. Maintain eye contact, sit quietly without fidgeting, and arrange your hands and arms in a nonthreatening way—uncrossed and relaxed. Don't frown, grimace, sigh, play with your hair, crack your knuckles, tap your fingers, yawn, adjust your clothing, roll your eyes, slouch your body, grit your teeth, chew gum, cross and uncross your legs, move too quickly, look alarmed, or make faces. Nod your head occasionally to indicate you understand the speaker. Remain attentive without appearing tense or threatened.

Listen

An important part of true listening is a mental exercise called bracketing, the temporary giving up or setting aside of one's own assumptions and prejudices to experience as far as possible the speaker's world from the inside (Peck, 1978, p. 73). The first thing to do when a parent with a problem comes to call is to listen. I personally have always had a very hard time listening. Impulsive and easily distracted, my mind has "a mind of its own." It could be wandering elsewhere, planning dinner, or making up a to-do list; I might be thinking of what I want to say in response or formulating the perfect solution to the problem being presented. I've learned the hard way that none of these approaches wins friends, influences people, *or* solves problems. Because I am also hearing impaired, I must overcome yet another set of challenges to effective listening. Men with mustaches and accents are my nemesis. If I lose the main idea, recovering it without appearing inept is difficult. I've also discovered that listening is a whole lot more than just hearing the words people are speaking. Their facial expressions, body language, and tone of voice can communicate volumes about their true feelings.

HELPFUL HINTS FOR BEING A GOOD LISTENER

- Do not respond with your own message by evaluating, sympathizing, giving your opinion, offering advice, analyzing, or questioning. If you must talk, simply report back what you heard in the message as well as the attitudes and the feelings that were expressed.

- Make occasional and appropriate verbal responses, such as "oh," "hmm," or "uh-huh," to confirm to the speaker that you are paying attention. Parents need to feel that you understand them both emotionally (e.g., their feelings of anger or fear) and intellectually (the actual words they are saying).

- Keep listening until there is a sign that the parent has finished speaking and is ready to listen to you.

- Take notes (if appropriate to the situation) to help you remember critical details of the conversation. Most parents with problems will be relieved to know that you are really listening to them and care enough to write it down.

Be Curious

Veteran contributing educator Kathy Hoedeman has some unique advice for dealing with difficult parents:

> Discover the power of curiosity. Don't decide ahead of time what you think a parent is going to say. Don't plan ahead of time how you are going to *defend* your position or what words you want to be sure you say. As much as it may feel like it,

this is not about you. It is about a parent or parents and a child and what they are thinking and feeling. So, be curious. Wonder about why they are angry or upset. Wonder about how they got the information that caused them to get emotional. Wonder about what experiences they have had with education in the past. Wonder about their relationships with their child and their family dynamics. "Everyone has a story." Once you know even a little piece of the story, you can begin to understand why someone is feeling these emotions that have you off balance. Stories often come out when you are curious.

When I take the "curious" approach, I become much more focused on listening as opposed to talking. I often think parents can see it in my face and feel it in the tone of my voice. I am not here to prove I am right and they are wrong, I am here to listen and try to understand. Sometimes they begin talking and when they realize I am actually listening the conversation goes in a completely different direction than either party anticipated.

Be Gentle

Gentleness and artfulness are among the most effective ways of defusing anger while at the same time giving you the opportunity to determine the real source of a parent's anger (Taylor & Wilson, 1997, p. 67). Gentleness connotes courtesy, refinement, serenity, civility, and patience. If you have an assertive and strong personality, cultivating gentleness may seem to be an artifice. But, you will be amazed to see how "a soft answer [can] turn away wrath, [whereas] a harsh word stirs up anger" (Proverbs 15:1, Revised Standard Version). The term *artfulness* suggests cleverness and skill, a talent you have cultivated and worked on. Believe me, being gentle in the face of a parent gone ballistic doesn't feel normal when you first try it. Defending, excusing, and accusing come far more readily to the surface of our feelings and actions.

The tone and quality of your voice are just as important as the words you speak. If you are hurried, hostile, defensive, or distracted, your voice will give you away immediately, and parents will judge you to be insincere, even if you are saying all the right things. A soft answer means that you don't contradict, correct, condescend, or disagree with parents who are already infuriated, even if they are misinformed. Don't be impatient or act harried.

Read Between the Lines

Management consultant Peter Drucker (2018) writes, "The most important thing in communication is hearing what isn't said." Infer and intuit. Sometimes people don't have the courage to say what they need or want to say. If you can decipher their intent and feed it back to them for confirmation, you can ease parents' fears and concerns without their having to fully articulate them. This is a tricky strategy and must be used with discretion.

Give "Wordless Advice"

It has taken me years of practice to perfect the art of giving what I call "wordless advice," not only with parents who are upset but with my own family members. I finally learned that when people come to me with a problem, they don't necessarily want my advice, they just want an empathetic ear. They don't want my eyes to glaze over and my mind to drift to personal agendas; they want my full attention and thoughtful nods and "hmms." They don't want me to talk "at" them either. They need a sounding board, a place to reason out their own problems. By the time they finish their monologues, they thank me for the great advice (I never said a word) and go merrily on their ways. Here's a summary of what you can do to become a better listener.

- Notice the attitudes and feelings of individuals. They may communicate something different from what their words are saying. Posture, eye movements, hand gestures, tone of voice, and facial expressions are powerful communicators.

- Listen "between the lines" for what a parent is not saying in addition to what is being said.

- Do not respond with your own message by evaluating, sympathizing, giving your opinion, offering advice, analyzing, or questioning. Simply report back what you heard in the message as well as the attitudes and the feelings that were expressed.

- Keep listening until there is a sign that the speaker has finished speaking and is ready to listen to you.

Use Mirroring

Mirroring is a form of feedback in which you repeat back *some* of the same words or phrases that another person is using (Brinkman & Kirschner, 1994, p. 45). Although paraphrasing (different from backtracking) is often recommended as a way of confirming that you have understood what someone is saying, perceptive people often resent having their words replaced by your words. To them, that implies that you're twisting the meaning of what they've said. In mirroring, you don't echo everything that is said but instead, focus on key words that capture the main idea. This will let parents know that you have heard and understood.

Open Your Mind

Parents who are troubled and frightened often need permission and acceptance from teachers to share their private and deeply felt concerns. If they sense that you aren't interested, don't care, or are passing premature judgment, they may well get cold feet and suddenly leave without articulating the real problem. Parents need the freedom to explore an issue without criticism or censure. In the process, you may be exposed to a new point of view or an alternative way of viewing education, so suspend your initial prejudice or distaste and become a learner.

Don't React

Reacting is acting without thinking. There are many possible ways to react that are inappropriate. Sometimes, our first inclination when cornered by an angry parent is to strike back (e.g., counterattack, defend, explain, justify, or just plain cut off and "divorce" parents we don't like). Instead, step back and remain neutral. Don't personalize the attack and try to convince the parent of their wrongness and your rightness. Equally ineffective is giving in just to get a parent out of your classroom *and* your life, without regard for the child or policies already in place to handle such situations. Be firm and stand your ground while solving problems. Having a reputation as a wimpy pushover is almost as bad as being labeled a terrible tyrant. Command respect. Neither run away from the problem nor gear up for battle.

Remain Composed

"To change a difficult person, you must first change yourself—your way of thinking about the person and your way of responding to the familiar provocations" (Tavris, 1978, p. 294). Most of us find it difficult to be neutral about parents who are angry and hostile. They bring out the worst in us. Maintaining your composure will effectively dismantle the hostile feedback loop that can be created if you respond in kind to angry words. As Tavris goes on to say,

> If you're pleasant and cordial, you will, in the long run, wear them down, even get them to be cordial back. It's surprising how often they warm up—not always, but often—because so often their hostility masks their own loneliness and insecurity. And in the long run, who benefits most by your being friendly and cordial? You do. (p. 299)

Your composure and courtesy will act as a mirror in which parents will find their own desperate attempts to intimidate and abuse embarrassingly and unattractively reflected.

When parents sense your confidence, and they will, their bluster and bravado will diminish. If they sense fear and uncertainty, they will take advantage of it every time.

Be Assertive

Inward feelings of negativity and low self-esteem can make it very difficult for you to handle angry parents. Cultivating positive feelings of self-esteem will enable you to manage your own anger more effectively when confronted by angry parents as well as to place their angry feelings in perspective. Angry and hostile parents are a little like dogs and horses. They sense when you are unsure or hesitant and will take over before you know it.

Administer Shock Therapy

If you are personally being browbeaten and bullied by parents, stop them in their tracks immediately with a firm assertion: "Mr. Flint, I can understand why you are so distressed. I would like to talk with you about how your child is being treated and make sure that it doesn't happen again. But, first you have to sit down, lower your voice, and stop swearing. At ABC School we always try to treat one another with respect. That's why we're not going to tolerate someone being rude to your son on the playground, and I can't tolerate rude behavior from you either. So, please calm down and let's begin all over again." Administering "shock therapy" can remind parents where they are, with whom they are speaking, and what their real priority is—their child (Axelrod & Holtje, 1997, p. 87).

Apologize

Sometimes, the first words from your mouth, when a parent stops talking long enough to come up for air, should be an apology. In these litigious days, many educators are loath to say they are sorry, fearing lawsuits and damages, but not saying you're sorry when you are obviously at fault will only exacerbate an already difficult situation. Often, if educators are willing to apologize, parents will back down and admit they or their child are also at fault.

Empathize

Learn to lay aside your own needs to be heard and understood, and instead focus on hearing and understanding what parents have to say. Perhaps, you have never had an experience identical to the one they are having, but suspend belief for a moment and imagine yourself in the parents' shoes. How would you feel? How would you act? Where would you go for help? Suppose your child was being evaluated for an intellectual disability. Would you be calm, trusting, and totally relaxed? I doubt it. Suppose your child was being bullied on the playground, and you thought no one cared. Would you take it lying down? Probably not. If you sincerely engage in this exercise of imagination, the parents with whom you are meeting will feel your empathy and begin to relax. I shudder with embarrassment when I think of a parent-teacher conference I had early in my teaching career. I had the temerity to suggest to the mother of nine children that *she* should spend at least 30 minutes every school night helping her fifth-grade son master his multiplication facts. I still remember the look of utter amazement she gave me. As a brand-new teacher I was long on enthusiasm but very short on empathy.

Welcome Criticism

To welcome criticism is to take the "Appreciate" car on the "A" Train. Perhaps the idea of welcoming criticism from parents or being appreciative for the bad news they bear is as attractive to you as the prospect of oral surgery. But sometimes we need to hear and heed what parents have to say that might help us improve how we deliver education to their children. And even when the criticism is more destructive than constructive, we need to listen and respond with openness, interest, and appreciation. John Foster Dulles (2004), the noted statesman, once said, "The measure of success is not whether you have a tough problem to deal with, but whether it is the same problem you had last year." If you have a steady stream of distressed parents complaining about the same issue (e.g., your homework policy or bullying in your classroom), it's time to address these issues and stop burying your head in the sand. The worst thing you can ever say to a parent who comes to you with a concern is, "You're the only parent who's ever complained about this." Even if the statement is true, it won't be for long when they get home and start phoning everyone on the class list.

If there's a problem, tell parents you'll investigate it, and thank them for bringing it to your attention. Then, start investigating.

Consider Cultural Differences

When the parents with whom you are meeting have a different cultural background than you do, try to understand the subtleties that characterize their nonverbal behaviors and communication patterns. Nonverbal signals to consider include distance between people, eye contact, and whether touching is expected or appropriate. Who should initiate the conversation, whether interrupting is acceptable, and how to bring up difficult topics are also important considerations. If you are aware of cultural differences, you can alter your behavior patterns to put parents at ease and increase the likelihood of productive problem solving.

If you are working with a translator, never address your remarks to the translator. He or she is merely a conduit. Maintain eye contact with the parents. Learn how to say hello, good-bye, thank you for coming, and I'll do all I can to help you in several languages if necessary.

Getting perpetrators to realize that they are acting in a biased manner is a monumental task, because (a) on a conscious level they see themselves as fair-minded individuals who would never consciously discriminate, (b) they are genuinely not aware of their biases, and (c) their self-image of being "a good moral human being" is assailed if they realize and acknowledge that they possess biased thoughts, attitudes, and feelings that harm people of color.

End Positively

At the close of the conference, summarize what you think you've heard. Not only is this a good-faith gesture that lets parents know you fully understand their point of view, but a brief review of critical information will clear up any misconceptions that may exist on either side of the table. Even if the meeting concludes without consensus, the knowledge that they have been heard and understood will defuse most angry parents and calm the most anxious ones. Be sure to keep careful notes of the action items for immediate follow-up.

HOW TO DEAL WITH VERY DYSFUNCTIONAL PARENTS

I wish I could promise a money-back guarantee that the aforementioned responsive strategies will produce positive feedback from parents. But, if you have tried them all and the storm clouds are still hovering, then it is likely you have encountered one of a small, but absolutely terrifying, group of parents that make even the most self-confident teachers shiver in their shoes. I have yet to meet the teacher who doesn't instantly relate to my choice of the term *crazy* to describe a small, often highly vocal group of parents. The parents who fall into this rare but very troubling category require careful handling. The strategies that work with parents who are merely angry, troubled, or afraid may or may not work with parents who are also abusive, dysfunctional, dishonest, or just on a "power trip" at school. These parents often require special handling.

The reasons for their behavior are almost always beyond your control, or even unknown to you. But, before you assume that nothing will work with out-of-control parents, give all or some of the aforementioned strategies a try. Just in case you come up short, here are some special strategies for "crazy" parents.

Marriages in Crisis

Consider yourself most fortunate as a teacher if the parents of your students who are having marital difficulties don't bring their disagreements to school. Most of the parents who fall into this category are able to handle the day-to-day stresses of breaking up a marriage, but the few who can't need special handling to keep their children on track in school.

"Breaking up is hard to do," and many couples seem to do it with hostility, venom, anger, temper tantrums, and even physical violence and damage to property. The minute the news *is* public, it's important for school personnel to be in the know—not as to who did what and when to whom, but to have a record of what types of custody agreements are in place, where children will be living and when, whether grandparents are involved, where to reach parents in case of emergencies, and whether any restraining orders have been issued by a judge. Teachers *must* do the legal thing. Unfortunately, the legal thing doesn't always seem to make sense, but ours is not to reason why.

Contributing educator Stacey May finds that divorced parents are sometimes difficult to handle. Conferences with them can become a juggling act of keep them focused and on track. Don't get too cozy with either mom or dad, or you could find yourself triangulated in a divorce case and be subpoenaed to testify. Be cautious in conversations, lest the education of their child become another source of contention or a bartering point for making the ex-partner feel inadequate. Offer a listening ear, and counsel regarding academic, behavioral, and social problems at school. Your role is to ensure children feel secure and safe at school. Politely decline to hear the particulars of a family's marital woes.

Abusive, Addictive, Violent, and Mentally Ill Parents

This category of parents needs *very* special handling *and* as much professional assistance as you have available. Here are the must-dos when dealing with abusive, addictive, violent, and mentally ill parents.

1. Gather as much information as you can about the parents to help you understand their behavior and motivations.

2. Make sure that you follow all of the rules when dealing with parents who live on the edge. The fact that parents are breaking them left and right should never tempt you to play their game.

3. Although you might suspect that parents are abusing drugs or alcohol, never accuse them. Call the police if you have any suspicions, and let them handle the situation. If possible, keep your classroom door open, and alert office personnel to a possible need for a 911 call.

4. Watch for physical signs of impending violence, such as clenched fists, agitated tone of voice, flared nostrils, red face, and wide-open eyes (Morgan, 2003, p. 44). If you have any reason to believe parents are carrying weapons into your school, call the police immediately, and have an emergency plan in place to evacuate the hallways and lock down the classrooms.

5. Keep careful and complete notes about all experiences and encounters with this category of parents. If you don't write it all down, later you may doubt that it ever happened. But more important, parents may begin to lie or contradict your version, and you will need records of what was said and when. In some cases, you might even need a witness to confirm that a letter was sent or a document delivered to parents.

6. Keep your department chairs, counselor, and all administrators informed. Never underestimate the power of a "crazy" parent to wreak havoc. Get there first with the facts. They will appreciate your early warning system.

7. Consult with mental health professionals. If you are dealing with a parent who has a documented problem, learn more about it, so you don't inadvertently say or do the wrong thing.

8. Consult with law enforcement officials in advance of a meeting, if possible. There have been occasions when I have asked for a police officer to be available in the school building during a conference with a potentially dangerous parent.

9. Know your school board policies, the legal rights of parents and students, and the requirements of your own job description. There will be parents who have read all of these documents and be waiting to trap you.

10. Invite someone else to attend the parent conference to take notes or to witness what is happening. Use the special skills of the counselor, social worker, or school psychologist to help you defuse an explosive situation.

11. Be aware of the laws protecting the rights of children and your legal obligation to report any abuse of a child in your classroom.

12. Also, be aware of any district policies or state laws that can protect you from dangerous parents.

13. Find a trusted colleague or superior with whom to discuss the problem and how you are handling it. Don't go it alone. Ask for advice and perspective, and then be prepared to follow through on suggestions, if they will help resolve the situation. Take care, however, to be discrete. The more individuals with whom you share your story, the more likely it will find its way back to the wrong person.

14. Don't take it personally. It may seem at times as though a highly dysfunctional parent's behavior is targeted specifically at you. If you have an opportunity to talk with the teachers or administrator at a school the child formerly attended, you will no doubt find similar behavior patterns.

15. Make sure that you know how to handle your own emotions, or you could make a difficult situation impossible.

Parents Who Are Missing in Action

There is a substantial group of parents who I would call missing in action. These parents may not express anger or any negative emotions toward you—and yet their lack of involvement presents its own unique challenges. They seem oblivious to the frequent missives you send home with their children. The children are often parenting their parents and will need lots of encouragement and support at school.

- Parents who are homeless or living in poverty may have few options for getting to your school. There are many occasions when districts determine boundary lines with convoluted and lengthy bus rides for children. They may be oblivious to the burdens placed on both teachers and parents when parents cannot walk to school or at the very least find reasonable public transportation.

- Parents who are addicted to drugs or alcohol may simply be too incapacitated or too embarrassed to make it to school for a conference.

- Some parents may suffer from agoraphobia and are anxious and fearful about going out in public. This condition makes it impossible for them to consider going to school for a conference with a teacher. These individuals are likewise fearful about agreeing to a home visit from a teacher.

USING YOUR ENCOUNTERS WITH PARENTS TO LEARN AND GROW

Buddhists believe that we can and should be grateful for everyone who crosses our path. That point of view is a difficult one to embrace when we've just been raked over the coals by an irate parent. Why should we be grateful for someone who's out to make our life miserable? Or so it seems. But if you look on each encounter with a parent, whether angry or dysfunctional, as an opportunity to learn and grow as a person and professional, you will find yourself developing an entirely different attitude about dealing with challenging and difficult parents. Sometimes, in the midst of the harsh words and angry tempers, you will learn patience and forbearance. Often, while you're enduring frustration and embarrassment, you will reach deep within and discover a gift for helping others to solve seemingly insoluble problems. You will learn to manage and channel your own feelings of anger and fear, and in your strength, you will be a resource to parents who need wise counsel more than ever. In the end, however, we do it for the children.

SUMMING UP AND LOOKING AHEAD

In Chapter 1 we explored the five facets of today's education landscape that can interact in unexpected and sometimes frightening ways. Chapter 2 provided you with more than two dozen proactive ways you can step out to meet, interact, and get parents on your side. This chapter peeled back some of the various layers of effective communication and offered more specific ways to deal with the most dysfunctional parents.

In the upcoming chapter you will find an overview of the most common types of problem situations found in schools. The chapter suggests some exploratory and action strategies to solve the problems and gradually begin to reduce the number of angry parent encounters you have during the course of a school year.

CHAPTER 4

SOLVING THE PROBLEMS THAT MAKE PARENTS ANGRY, TROUBLED, AFRAID, AND SEEM EVEN CRAZIER

The mere formulation of a problem is far more often essential than its solution.

—Albert Einstein (n.d.)

Defusing and disarming the emotionally charged parents who arrive at your class-room door is only the first step. Once a *real* problem is identified and *hopefully* agreed upon, it's time to use the exploratory and action strategies found in this chapter to help solve the problem(s) that are the source of parents' anger, fear, and distress. I do hope that you love problems if you have chosen a career in education, for if you don't, you no doubt face a measure of trepidation every day, wondering when you'll receive the next phone call or visit from a distressed parent. But, don't ever let the members of your parent community get the feeling that you don't want to hear bad news. Soon, everyone but you will know "the sky is falling." If you are guilty of any of the following behaviors, become more receptive and open to hearing about potential problems and difficult situations. Forewarned is forearmed.

- Do you subtly discourage parents from rocking the boat or bringing bad news to your attention?

- Do you avoid asking open-ended questions of students and parents, such as "How are things going?" or "Are you feeling good about school this year?" for fear that you might get an answer you won't like?

- Do you keep your schedule so tightly structured that you never seem to have time to schedule a parent conference?

- Do you procrastinate when it comes to returning parent phone calls or replying to text messages and emails in a timely way?

THE PERVASIVE PROBLEMS THAT WILL PLAGUE YOU

School problems come in all shapes and sizes. They occur in the classroom, on the play-ground, in the lunchroom, and on the bus. Sometimes, students notice them first, or parents call you with a concern. But more often than not, you identify the problems at school and then have to decide how best to resolve them. School problems that are ignored or left unre-solved can result in unhappy parents, and when parents are upset, chances are their children will be doing less than their best in school.

For purposes of this discussion, a school problem is defined as anything that keeps a child from achieving his or her learning potential. Sometimes, school problems can be solved with a phone call or a brief parent-teacher conference. Sometimes, a long-term, comprehensive intervention plan is needed. But if ignored, a real school problem can grow like an out-of-control weed, choking communication between home and school, cutting off trust and cooperation, and stifling the academic growth of the student. Let's look at the three major sources of school problems in more detail.

Problems Identified by School Personnel

Educators specialize in identifying problems, although I've often felt like we're much better at finding them than solving them. Skilled teachers can often identify several children with problems before the first week of school is over. The best teachers give children some time to settle in, do what they can to solve a problem at school, and then notify parents that all is not well.

The concern may come in the form of a telephone call, an email, or a formal report card. The phrases are usually polite and couched in educational jargon, but the meaning is quite clear to parents: "Your child isn't measuring up to some standard of behavior or achievement, and you as a parent need to do something about it."

"Mary seems a bit immature with regard to her social relationships."

"I'm concerned about John's behavior. He isn't following our classroom rules, and none of my usual strategies seem to be working."

"Sarah is falling behind in her work. She has failed the last two math tests, and if she doesn't spend more time studying for the next quiz, she might receive a failing grade."

"Your daughter can't seem to get along with anyone. She wants her own way no matter what the situation."

"We're concerned about a possible learning problem with your son, Jeremy. Could you call and make an appointment for a conference at your earliest convenience?"

"Jessica doesn't seem quite ready for first grade. She hasn't learned her letter sounds and often has a difficult time paying attention when we read stories in the circle."

"Ken hasn't turned in his science homework for over a week. Can you give me a call right away?"

It took me a while to realize that the majority of parents have done the very best they know how. It's not as if they purposely raised a child who can't or won't learn or tried to bring up their offspring to break all the rules in the book. So, when they are faced with the prospect of their child's problems in school, their stomachs tighten into knots, they relive their own failures as students, and they immediately launch into a cycle of self-blame and recrimination or adopt a defensive position that lays the blame squarely on someone else. That someone else would be you, the teacher. For parents, finding solutions to the problems with which teachers confront them usually involves facing difficult truths and choices about themselves and their children, often requires large investments of time (and money) on the part of everyone involved, and may mean substantial changes in attitudes and behaviors. Tough choices. Hard work.

Problems Identified by Students

The final category of school problems centers on issues identified by the students themselves. If parents are regularly talking with their children and listening to what they say, there are often clues regarding potential problems in their comments.

"The teacher doesn't like me."

"I don't understand a thing that's going on in that class."

"I got a D on my last math test."

"Nobody likes me."

"My lunch was stolen out of my locker."

"I got put back in a lower reading group today."

"I'm in the dumb class."

"I don't understand my homework."

All children complain about school occasionally. Learning to distinguish between a real problem and the everyday ups and downs of life at school is a critical skill for teachers (and parents). Every school day will not run smoothly for every child, and part of growing up is learning to deal with our imperfect world. But when the complaints are constant and revolve around a central theme, or when they begin to affect appetite, sleep habits, or personality, that's a warning that a serious school problem is in the making (McEwan, 1992). Don't try to pass off complaints as unimportant or a figment of a child's imagination. My experiences as a parent, teacher, and administrator have shown me that children are sensitive human beings with important perceptions about their schooling experiences. If for any reason they aren't happy in school, we need to do all we can to get to the bottom of their anxieties. Any problem faced by a child at school is a real problem that must be addressed. Sometimes, all we need to do is listen and empathize.

SOLVING THE PROBLEMS THAT PLAGUE YOU

Listening, empathizing, and apologizing are always helpful when meeting with parents, but eventually you are expected to solve some of the problems that brought those angry parents to your classroom in the first place. Oh, you don't have to solve these problems single-handedly. That is never wise. But as a child's teacher, you have considerable power to gather information, marshal resources, convene meetings, and facilitate problem solving— that is, to implement the exploratory and action strategies. Without your involvement and expertise, most school problems will just fester and worsen.

Exploratory Strategies

During the exploration phase of an encounter with an upset parent, seek to gather more information, understand the problem more completely, and casually offer some possible options. This phase will likely begin during your initial meeting with parents and if necessary continue to a second meeting devoted completely to problem solving.

Take Your Time

There is no rule that says every problem needs an immediate solution. Always take time to think; any decision (or upset parent) will benefit from a 24-hour cooling-off period. Never permit parents to back you into the "I've got to know what you're going to do now" corner. "The wise [teacher] knows how to create baffles and buffers to buy time, to absorb heat, to promote collective wisdom, to insure a maximum sense of legitimacy for final decisions" (Bailey, 1971, p. 225). Here are some ways to slow down the action:

- During the meeting, pause and say nothing, to give yourself time to gather your thoughts. During a long pause, you can sip your water or check your notes.

- Regroup by taking a few minutes to summarize the information or progress made thus far.

- Never commit to or even suggest an action that involves other individuals (especially other teachers) without first consulting with them.

- Ask for time to gather more information or to consult with your administrator. This sends the message that you are serious about solving the problem and want to make sure you're fully informed.

- When a meeting is headed nowhere (e.g., information is being repeated, tempers are beginning to flare, and nothing is being accomplished), perhaps it's time to schedule a follow-up meeting. Consider including some experts (e.g., a behavior management specialist to discuss some ways to improve time on task in the classroom, or the librarian to explain the book selection policy of the district) to help defuse the situation.

Ask Questions

Learn the power of asking the right questions to uncover all aspects of a problem. This process can be compared to the party gag of putting a small gift-wrapped box in increasingly larger and larger boxes, wrapping each one more elaborately than the last. Just when the person who is doing the unwrapping thinks he's about to get his "real" present, he discovers that the final box is empty. Sometimes in talking with parents, a similar phenomenon will occur. Once all of the layers of confusion and misinformation have been peeled away, the problem may be nonexistent.

Ask all of the usual "who, what, where, and why" questions. You may also find it helpful to use statements such as "I'm not sure I understand. Help me to see why this is so important to you." Offer alternative ways of thinking in the form of questions such as these: "Might it work this way?" or "What if we tried this approach?" When all else fails, ask for the parents' advice: "If you were in my place, what would you do?" or "Do you really think that would be a fair way of handling this problem?" Don't be afraid of asking open-ended questions to which you have no suitable answers. But beware of assuming the role of prosecuting attorney in your questioning mode. Clarification, not conviction, is your ultimate goal. There are a number of positive things that can happen as you question parents with whom you're meeting (Brinkman & Kirschner, 1994, p. 46):

You will gather higher-quality information than what has been offered.

You can help the other person become more rational.

You can patiently and supportively demonstrate that you care about what the parent is saying.

You can slow a situation down long enough to see where it's heading.

You can surface hidden agendas and reveal misinformation without being adversarial.

Sometimes, strange and surprising things can happen if you are able to lay aside your own mental models (or paradigms) and consider alternatives. Mental models are "the images, assumptions, and stories that we carry in our minds of ourselves, other people, institutions, and every aspect of the world. Like a pane of glass framing and subtly distorting our vision, mental models determine what we see" (Senge, Kleiner, Roberts, Ross, & Smith, 1994, p. 235). Senge and colleagues offer a variety of conversational recipes for turning encounters with people who are challenging or disagreeing with us into a discovery of their mental mode. For example, when faced with an impasse, they advise asking questions such as "Are we starting from two very different sets of assumptions here? Where do they come from?" or "It feels like we're getting into an impasse, and I'm afraid we might walk away without any better understanding. Have you got any ideas that will help us clarify our thinking?" (pp. 200–201). The notion that a conference with a distressed parent might actually turn out to be a learning experience for you as the teacher may be a somewhat revolutionary idea to consider, but drop your defenses and give it a try.

Chris Argyris (1986, 1991), the noted organizational theorist, suggests that most skilled people in day-to-day communication must "unlearn" how to protect themselves from being threatened before they can ever become truly effective managers. I submit that this statement holds true for teachers as well. Teachers are well and truly managers of fairly complex mini-enterprises—managing the behavior and learning of dozens of children and communicating with all of their parents.

Open the Option Door

Use verbal aikido techniques, similar to those used in martial arts (Crowe, 1999). Aikido practitioners don't stiffen their bodies in resistance when an opponent comes at them. Rather they move forward and down, taking the "wind out of the sails" of their opposition and diluting the force and effects of a bodily thrust. Rather than telling parents what they can't have or what you won't be able to do for them because of your policies and procedures, suggest some possible options that *might* work. Of course, you will need to be quick thinking, lest you make promises you can't keep, but experience helps, and so does asking for time to explore and examine some possible options. Use phrases like the following to "open the option door" (Crowe, 1999, p. 173):

Here are some options . . .

- What I *can* tell you is. . . .
- What you *can* do is. . . .

- Which would you rather have?
- Give me some specifics so that I can see how to help you.
- Have you tried. . . .

Undersell and Overperform

This is a classic principle from the world of business (Axelrod & Holtje, 1997), but it also has applications in your dealings with upset parents. Promise far less than you think you can deliver. If a parent wants a child moved out of your team member's room because her son gets stomach aches during her math lessons, don't even suggest the possibility that moving him to another classroom is an option. That solution involves too many moving parts over which you have no control.

Lower the Boom Lightly

There is an art to giving negative news, something you may well be called on to do in the course of meeting with parents who are upset. How do you tell parents that their child is a bully? How do you share the possibility that a child may have a severe learning disability? How do you communicate with parents who want to blame everything on you when they own a big share of the problem? Very carefully. With tact and gentleness. But with directness. Don't be so afraid of telling the truth that you never get to the point. Gauge how much information parents can comprehend at one time, particularly if the information is coming as a complete surprise to them. Don't babble and generalize. Speak simply and give concrete examples.

Focus on Problems, Not Personalities

Stay focused on issues, and keep people and their flaws and faults out of the discussion as much as possible. When parents start tearing you down, try to redirect their attention to solving the problem.

Action Strategies

For those of you who are action oriented, employing the responsive and exploratory strategies can seem like wasted time in a sense. We feel like we already know the answers and need to get on with it. There may be many instances when that is the case. Parents are reasonable, the problem is a small one, and everyone agrees regarding the solution. However, when parents are angry, troubled, afraid, and especially just plain dysfunctional, taking the time to respond and explore is time well spent. Rushing to judgment and action can exacerbate a bad situation, especially if you end up solving the wrong problem. We are, however, finally at the point of getting down to business. Here are the action strategies you've been waiting for.

Solve Problems

The characteristics of good problem solvers are amazingly similar to the qualities one needs to be a good parent or marriage partner: patience, discipline, creativity, honesty, and continuous learning (Lynch & Werner, 1992, p. 160). Problem solving is always a part of quality decision making, but solutions do not come without struggle, frustration, and occasional bouts of chaos and messiness from time to time. Every theorist has developed his or her own model of problem solving, but most include some variation of these seven steps as "must-dos":

1. **Gather all the facts and define the problem.** Rushing to judgment or stating your opinion about a situation before you have listened to the various sides will often result in solving the wrong problem. Very few educational problems need immediate solutions, and the more information you have at your fingertips, the more likely that a quality solution will present itself. Some possible sources of information include observations, test scores, historical data, and consultations with a variety of specialists. Find someone on your student support team whom you trust, and use that individual as a sounding board for thinking out loud.

2. **Identify some possible reasons for or sources of the problem.** Beware of responding too quickly with your own expertise. You may know exactly what is needed, but even if you are absolutely correct in your assessment, the parents will need time to reach the same conclusion. I've worked with parents who needed several months to recognize what was best for their child, and if we had not given them that time and space, we would have frustrated our ultimate goal of helping the child.

3. **Verify the most likely causes.** Sometimes, finding a cause is impossible and a waste of everyone's time. In other situations, determining the cause is a guarantee of a quick solution.

4. **Identify several possible solutions.** Rare is the problem that has only one solution (even in math), so don't get committed to your solution too early in the discussion. You will shut down the creativity of others and may miss the best one. On the way to determining a solution to the problem, avoid blaming the child, the parents, or yourself. Assigning blame is counterproductive and anger evoking. Assume that you all did the best you knew how up to that point. If behavioral changes (in parent, teacher, student) are called for, someone (with administrative know-how and leadership) will have to provide help for the needy parties (e.g., staff development, behavior management support, parent training, counseling). Just *telling* people to change (whether parents, students, *or* teachers) doesn't work.

5. **Determine the solution that seems best, and then develop an action plan to implement it.** An important part of developing the action plan is to make sure that all of the participants know the why, who, what, where, and when of the plan. I have seen many wonderful plans fail for lack of accountability. Everyone should know why the plan has been designed (e.g., to improve homework completion, to raise reading achievement, or to improve a student's time on task). All of the participants (who) should know the exact actions (what) they're supposed to take. Put the behavioral expectations in writing, and make sure everyone has a copy, including the child. Include a time line in the plan (when), and also include the location (where) in which the activities will occur. Anything that is left to chance will not happen.

6. **Implement the plan.** Make sure you give the plan enough time to work.

7. **Evaluate and fine-tune the plan.** Look for concrete evidence of success (e.g., more assignments turned in, fewer unacceptable behaviors, more positive interactions between parent and teacher).

Be forewarned that as you move through the problem-solving process, there are three possible scenarios that can occur: consensus, compromise, and confrontation-capitulation.

If *consensus* is reached, all the players (parent, teacher, and especially the child) agree on the nature of the problem and the solution. There could be some minor differences but not enough to hinder solving the problem. Parents are supportive of school personnel's plans, and they are going to do everything they can at home to help. Sharon's case is a perfect example of consensus and collaboration. Everyone agreed that Sharon had a serious problem. She was in third grade and didn't know how to read. She had transferred in from a private school, where her learning problems had fallen through the cracks due to constant turnover in teaching personnel during her first-grade year. Her new teacher quickly recognized Sharon's reading disability and referred her for testing. It was clear that she had a learning disability. We immediately gave her special services and prescribed activities for her parents to do at home. We also talked with Sharon about what her part would be. Everyone followed through and we all did our part, and by sixth grade, Sharon was reading above grade level and winning awards in reading. Not every problem has such a successful resolution, but it is an example of what can happen when everyone, including the child, cooperates to solve the problem.

Sometimes, there is disagreement as to the nature of the problem or the type of solution that is needed. In that case, a *compromise* may be reached. Both parents and school personnel agree to disagree on one or more issues but do so in the spirit of cooperation and together are able to work for what is best for the child. Compromise was the result of a problem-solving conference held with Mr. and Mrs. Stafford and their sixth-grade daughter, Joanna. Joanna had a serious personality conflict with a newly assigned teacher (hired to replace a teacher on maternity leave), and the situation had gone from bad to worse. The new teacher felt that Joanna was an indulged and spoiled adolescent. Her parents felt the new teacher was incompetent. Joanna was driving a wedge between the school and her parents. The principal was caught in the middle. The Staffords wanted an immediate change in her placement but agreed to a temporary plan designed by the teacher, the principal, and Joanna. There wasn't complete support from home, but the Staffords agreed to wait and see before pressing the transfer issue any further. We managed to make it to the end of the school year without bloodshed.

When there is no agreement and little promise for consensus or even compromise, the result is *confrontation or capitulation* or both. If a parent wants a course of action to be taken that school personnel do not find acceptable, or school personnel want a course of action to be taken that parents cannot support, an impasse is the result. Effective administrators and teachers always keep looking for ways to solve problems, but if an administrator is unwilling to negotiate or a parent is intractable, capitulation is the only answer. Although this is clearly a last resort, finding another schooling option for a child may be the only solution. Remember, however, that the goal of problem solving is to find a way to help each child be successful in the academic, behavioral, and social arenas.

A SHORT LIST OF THINGS NOT TO DO DURING A PROBLEM-SOLVING SESSION

There are several responses you might make to parents who are upset that will backfire on you. Here's the short list of things not to do:

- Don't interrupt. Sit on your hands. Bite your tongue. Even if the person who's talking has made a mistake, don't jump in to correct it.

- Don't take over the conversation in an attempt to keep from hearing about a problem.

- Don't try to change the subject without giving notice that you're about to do so. Because my mind always seems to race off on my own personal tangents during conversations, I fight this no-no vigorously. When I do feel compelled to veer sharply from the agenda, I give the time-out signal from football and warn the person with whom I'm speaking. But to someone who's upset, changing the subject is highly inflammatory.

- Never focus on things that can't be changed. Concentrate on the alterable variables over which you and the parent have control. Never start complaining about your own agenda (e.g., attacking the superintendent or board of education for not giving you enough money to have the programs you want).

- Don't engage in silent combat (e.g., trying to stare the person down without saying a word).

- Don't start rehearsing your answer before you've actually heard and understood what the parent is trying to communicate.

- Don't advise unless you're asked.

- Don't try to persuade parents by implying or stating that you are right and they are wrong.

- Don't try so hard to be neutral that you show no empathy.

- Don't come across as the know-it-all professional.

- Don't talk compulsively and overexplain, or you will raise questions in the minds of your listeners.

- Don't let yourself get backed into a corner by a parent who intimidates you. Think before you say "yes" or "no."

- Don't be so intent on smoothing a conflict that you achieve only a superficial resolution.

SUMMING UP AND LOOKING AHEAD

In Chapters 2–4, we focused on two "big" ways educators can deal with parents who are angry, troubled, afraid, or just seem crazy: (1) we can help to defuse their emotions, and (2) we can facilitate solutions to their problems. But there are also proactive steps you can take to reduce or eliminate out-of-control emotions and problem situations in advance. Chapter 5 summarizes advice and wisdom contributed by experienced teachers about how they proactively keep parents happy.

CHAPTER 5

ADVICE FROM TEACHERS WHO HAVE SEEN IT ALL

The proactive approach to a mistake is to acknowledge it instantly, correct and learn from it.

—Stephen Covey (n.d.)

When you find yourself reflecting at length about a recent disturbing encounter with an angry or dysfunctional parent, there is no one who can understand what you are facing and then give you some commonsense wisdom like a colleague who has been there, done that, and survived. Once you have been through an explosive conference with a parent, there is only one question to ask yourself: *What can I learn from this experience?*

Everyone is a novice at the beginning of a teaching career. An encounter with an angry, troubled, fearful, or completely dysfunctional parent almost always comes out of the blue and is just like a gut punch. Voices are raised, accusations are made, your motives are maligned, and your expertise is demeaned. The whole process takes your breath away. You may suddenly find yourself reacting with anger, fear, or defensiveness. You may begin to doubt your decision to become an educator, thinking, "I signed up to be a teacher, not a punching bag for irate parents." You can only spend 24 hours feeling depressed and defeated. The true professionals very shortly begin to go proactive. They consult colleagues and develop routines and procedures that will enable them to more deeply understand where parents may be coming from and force them to become better communicators— teachers who are usually ahead of difficult parents.

Just ahead, experienced teachers eloquently describe the traumatic encounters they will never forget. Hopefully their experiences will reassure you that it's not just you. You aren't the only teacher who has ended up in tears for how unjustly you have been treated by an out-of-control parent. They have asked the hard questions and will tell you what they learned from their experiences.

DEALING WITH PARENTS WHOSE PROBLEMS YOU CAN'T SOLVE: STACEY MAY

I remember meeting with a set of parents who were concerned that their child was not achieving to the standards that they thought he should be. They definitely felt that he should be getting much higher grades than he was. And, they had put their finger on the problem: my attitude. Rather than accepting that their child had not submitted work that was due and was very talkative and loud in class, they proceeded to blame me for being prejudiced against their child's religious beliefs. I calmly explained that it wasn't my role to judge the religious beliefs of their family. It was my job to help their child progress to meet academic standards. I managed to handle their first accusation with a measure of calm.

They then moved on to accuse me of not teaching the correct content. By this stage, I was feeling quite uncomfortable. I pointed them to the syllabus document and explained that what was in my program came directly from the syllabus and that it had been endorsed by our governing state authority. When my answers did not seem to suffice for them, I suggested that perhaps they should make an appointment with the principal or vice principal to discuss the matter further. After they left, I was so shaken that I went outside and cried.

What did Stacey learn from this experience?

What I wish I had known then is that the conversation was never really about me or the student (which is often the case). There were assumptions made by the parents and some wounds in other areas of their lives that were playing out in the interview. I wish I had known ahead of time that I would never be able to solve this problem and convince them of my educational expertise.

There are very few experienced teachers who cannot remember their first experience with a scary parent. Karen Rogers recently retired after 35 years of teaching. She has multiple degrees and certifications, but no amount of coursework can really ever prepare you for the first time you are blindsided by the anger of an upset parent. Karen Rogers can still recount in vivid detail her first experience with an out-of-control hostile father. Here is her story:

DEALING WITH A FEARFUL AND TROUBLED PARENT: KAREN ROGERS

Early on in my years of teaching right out of college I encountered a hostile father who yelled and screamed obscenities at me and told me I wasn't fit to teach his son.

Thankfully my principal and the counselor were present at the conference. We had asked for the meeting, since this man's child had become lethargic, moody, angry, and defiant. After I made several attempts to meet with the mother, we requested a conference with both parents attending. The dad showed up, and he was verbally abusive and extremely angry. He called me names because I did not have children of my own at the time. He stormed out before anyone could even speak to him about the issues we needed to address. This experience made me very nervous about upcoming parent-teacher conferences. I was a brand-new teacher and could not help but think that every meeting would be as stressful as this one. But I had support in the room and afterwards found out that the child was being abused. The father moved out of the home. In spite of the distress for me, I was glad we had addressed the situation and hopefully had made a positive difference for the boy and his mother.

(Continued)

(Continued)

What did Karen learn from this experience?

At that point Karen felt she had reached a crossroads in her teaching career. She determined to be proactive rather than reactive. She explains,

It was at this point that I decided to develop an agenda to use in every parent meeting. Having a set of specific steps that I would follow and a miniscript of some key things I wanted to say helped me feel more confident and usually defused any angry and troubled parents. During my many years as an educator, I have managed to positively interact and deal with a fair number of addicted and abusive parents. I have not only learned from these difficult parents, but have also been privileged to work with many positive and supportive parents who taught me valuable communication strategies.

Here are just a few of Karen's communication techniques:

- Make eye contact with the parents.
- Shake their hands firmly and give them a warm smile.
- Begin the conversation by saying something positive. Think ahead of time about how you might highlight one or two of the child's gifts.
- Let parents know that you care for the welfare of their child and your concern is the reason for the conference.
- Listen to what parents have to say.
- Try never to interrupt them, but listen to them respectfully.
- Never give parents any reason to think you are superior to them or know more than they do.
- Help parents to understand that their child is unique and important to you.
- Communicate a desire to learn from parents as you hope they might learn from you.

DEALING WITH AN ANGRY PARENT WHOSE CHILD IS UNDERPERFORMING: ANDREW LUCAS

My first encounter with an angry parent involved a young man whose mother thought he was underperforming. From my perspective, he struggled in math even though he paid attention in class. His homework was done consistently, and he participated in class discussions. Even so, he was a consistent high B student. This was not good enough for his mother, who insisted that he should be achieving at least an A. Being a young teacher and, consequently, being omniscient, I insisted that her expectations were too high. I can still remember the anger on her face during the parent meeting.

What did Andrew learn from this experience?

My principal took my side, but with the benefit of time and becoming a parent myself, I am now able to reflect on and understand her position. I'm not sure what else I could have done for that young man, but I certainly could have empathized more genuinely with his mother. Most likely there are also ways that I could have worked harder to ensure that he understood the material rather than taking an "I taught it, so you should have learned it" stance.

DEALING WITH PARENTS WHO REFUSE TO ACCEPT THE TRUTH ABOUT THEIR CHILD: JILLIAN D'ANGELO

One of my earliest experiences with difficult parents happened during my student teaching year in a fifth-grade classroom at a Catholic school. There was a student whose classroom performance, both during that present school year and prior years, indicated that he qualified for cognitive testing for at least two diagnoses: attention deficit disorder and some type of learning disability. In short, the student was failing fifth grade. The parents had a reputation for being difficult, so when the meeting to discuss the student's lack of progress was scheduled, the principal decided to have the entire fifth-grade teaching team present along with the school psychologist who coordinated student testing. The teachers presented the data to the parents as clearly as possible, explaining what the grade-level expectations were and where the student was falling short. We provided examples of Tier-1 (in the classroom) interventions that we had tried that had not been helpful in getting the student back on track. We discussed that with proper testing, a diagnosis, and an IEP, the student would be able to have certain accommodations that would help him be more successful.

(Continued)

(Continued)

The parents listened to all of this information, and then the dad responded, "Well, I simply disagree. We do not see these behavior problems at home. I think this is just a 10-year-old boy being a 10-year-old boy, and we refuse to have him tested." The situation was complicated by the fact that in the Catholic school system the school cannot provide an IEP or accommodation services without the parents agreeing to have the student tested as a preliminary measure. Without their agreement to begin that process, the teaching staff could do nothing except continue the school year as best we could. When the parents left the unproductive meeting, we all sighed. The school psychologist said what turned out to be the most powerful lesson of my student teaching experience, "Well, you can't care more than the parents." I was disturbed by her attitude. It seemed somewhat fatalistic and cynical to me, but I was just a student teacher and no one was asking for my opinion.

What did Jillian learn from this experience?

The meeting probably would have had a different outcome had it been handled differently. I think having the entire teaching team and the school psychologist there probably made the parents feel outnumbered and attacked right away. And I think that rather than starting the meeting with our list of complaints about the student, we should have heard what the parents had to say first. Making sure the parents feel heard is vital in setting a cooperative tone for any meeting. Although it is true that at some point if the parents are absolutely refusing to let you help their child ("I don't want him to receive any accommodations, I don't want him to be treated differently from anyone else in class") there is not much as a teacher that you can do. But I think it is more helpful to walk into these discussions with the view that both parent and teacher have the same goal of helping the child, and it is just a matter of finding a way that works for both parties, rather than having the fatalistic view of "nothing can be done."

Jillian continued to think about this meeting, and several years later discovered what she was looking for in a professional development opportunity taught by a corporate mediator: a simple step-by-step process to use when meeting with difficult, demanding, or confrontational parents.

Several years later, at a different school, the principal coordinated a professional development day led by an experienced corporate mediator. She taught the staff a step-by-step process we could use when meeting with difficult, demanding, or confrontational parents. It involved restating the demands of the parent; this strategy makes the parent feel heard and understood, as well as having the added benefit of helping them hear out loud particularly ridiculous demands that they may have brought up without thinking them through. The next step is to state, "I'm going to tell you what I can do, and what I can't do." State for the parents the things you are going to be able to do, such as, "I can sign off on Bobby's assignment notebook every afternoon to make sure he has written down the correct assignments. I can update the class website daily so that you and Bobby are able to see exactly what the homework is every night." Then after hopefully appeasing some of their demands, you lay down your boundaries of what is not possible. "I can't forgive Bobby's consequences when he forgets his assignments. He will lose points in his citizenship grade for each assignment that is turned in late."

The script we learned that day was not revolutionary; what made it so meaningful for me was to have a strategy when entering into a meeting, so that it did not devolve into unproductive complaining marathons from the parents. It helped me focus my thoughts during conferences and steer the conversation toward positive future steps rather than simply trying to defend my instructional decisions against criticism.

DEALING WITH A VERY ANGRY PARENT: JUSTIN GREMBA

The dad was sitting next to me at a parent conference. We had just started the meeting, and the parents were concerned about bullying. Their sixth-grade son liked to keep to himself and tended to get emotional when things didn't go his way. I assured the parents that we would not tolerate bullying in our classroom. The dad's response was to bite my head off. He screamed at me and his face was no more than an inch from mine.

I didn't move. Frozen from the shock of the moment, I waited until he was done. I then assured him that I was sorry if he felt that way, but I promised him that my teammates and I would not allow his son to be mistreated in any way during the rest of the school year. The remainder of the meeting was productive, and everybody left feeling as though they were heard.

(Continued)

(Continued)

The year progressed, and there were no longer any reports of bullying. The student was identified as needing emotional support and did have his fair share of problems during the remainder of the year, but there was no bullying. As the year neared its conclusion, I started to get emails from the dad offering me tickets to the various college and professional sporting events. Of course I could not accept these expensive gifts. Each email was extremely polite, friendly, and [appreciative] of everything we did for his son during the year.

What did Justin learn from this experience?

I know that the dad was upset because he saw his son being mistreated. After hearing his concerns and letting him know we would make sure his son was okay, he was able to let go of his anger and move toward appreciation of other adults looking out for his boy. Sometimes parents just need to feel as though they are being heard.

DEALING WITH THE PARENT OF A VERY CHALLENGING STUDENT: ROBYN ROSS

Robyn Ross has had her share of work with challenging parents over her 18 years of teaching. She has several gems of wisdom that she has polished over time. Here's one instance in which Robyn established a smooth working relationship between a difficult student and her parents.

Recently, a difficult student was transferred from another classroom to mine with the understanding that we were giving her a fresh start, so she could become successful for the remainder of the year. This change happened in the beginning of February. I was given a week's notice of this change, so the first thing I did was call and talk to the child's mom. I knew the child's reputation and had heard many stories, but I wanted to start a relationship with the parent on a positive note, because I knew she would be my biggest resource for information and follow-through at home. I asked simple questions that provided me with a wealth of information about this student who was about to become part of our classroom community.

1. What are your daughter's strengths?

2. What areas do you see as room for growth?

3. Does she have certain things or triggers that set her off?

4. What are your goals for her through this transition?

5. What else do you want me to know about your daughter?

At the end of my conversation with the mother, I promised to touch base frequently and keep her updated about how the transition was going. The first day my new student was in the classroom was the expected "honeymoon" period, so I jumped on that as an opportunity to send a positive email to mom. Every email that I subsequently sent noted positive things as well as areas for growth. Working with this student and parent has been a team effort to help the student be successful, and thankfully she has been.

What did Robyn learn from this experience?

Robyn recommends "going the extra mile" with the parents of especially challenging students.

Be willing to extend communication beyond what might be perceived as "normal" boundaries. For example, I send a weekly check-in email regarding one student, and another parent wants an email when things are going "sideways" at school. With both of these families, I have the freedom to write a note or send an email asking if there is anything going on at home that might be influencing certain behaviors that I am seeing at school. Usually there is a correlation. I also have two students working on specific goals in class for whom a check-in chart goes home daily and is signed and returned the following day. I could not implement these kinds of tailor-made plans without working with the parents to build open communication from the start of the year.

DEALING WITH A PARENT WHO THINKS I'M A SEXIST RACIST: ANDREW LUCAS

This encounter involved the parent of a child who insisted that her daughter should be able to skip a math course. Unfortunately, the data from her previous course, feedback

(Continued)

(Continued)

from her current teacher, and her performance on our placement test all indicated that she was best placed where she was. I presented all of this to the mother and to the advocate that she brought to the meeting. She stated her belief that I was denying her request because I was a sexist and a racist. Somehow, I maintained my composure and was able to show her data that said we had at that time proportional representation from females in the accelerated classes. She was still unhappy with me, but our interactions were always more amicable afterward.

What did Andrew learn from this experience?

Personally, this interaction (as well as the birth of my two daughters) has made me more sensitive to how I relate to the girls in my classroom. The parent was most certainly incorrect in her accusation, but it was something I had just never thought of directly before. Since that meeting, I have done my best to ensure that my math classroom is a place where both boys and girls feel safe to excel.

DEALING WITH AN OVERPROTECTIVE HELICOPTER PARENT: CINDY RICHARDSON

A difficult parent experience that still resonates for Cindy Richardson involved an over-protective parent of an only child. Here is Cindy's story:

The woman took her seat next to her husband and waited for the meeting to begin. No idle chitchat as with other parents; it appeared as if she would rather be anyplace but sitting in this Back-to-School parent meeting. I learned she was sending her only child to kindergarten and was nervous about the separation and possible anxiety her daughter might experience. Attempting to engage parents and help them feel at ease with the families of their child's classmates, I invite parents to introduce themselves and share a favorite thing about their child. This informal introduction gives me insight into family dynamics in addition to individual students.

I continued the meeting, explaining my classroom management procedures and expectations for our year together. I share my classroom motto, "Mistakes are for learning." While explaining the rubric for weekly behavior reports, I pointed out that no child is perfect, and most likely this will be a year of much social growth. I went on to say, "We want to learn a lot, so typically many mistakes will be made. Learning to share, asking for and granting forgiveness, and understanding the difference between reporting important information and tattling will take teaching and training for all students. Finding a balance between talking and listening, waiting patiently and engaging in activity, self-control and self-expression is unique to each child. It will take us a few weeks to settle into classroom expectations."

I moved on to other pertinent information; only the mother didn't. She was stuck, and unbeknownst to me, embarrassed. "She's perfect" was the favorite thing she'd shared about her child. I had unknowingly offended her by saying no child is perfect. She had no idea it was my standard "speech," and she felt singled out. Apparently, once the year was underway, no matter what I did, I never seemed to please this picky, overprotective parent. She was keeping a list of my offenses and requested a meeting facilitated by the principal in November. Prior to the meeting I racked my brain, trying to think of what I could have done to offend these parents enough to request this meeting with the principal. I attempted to keep my mouth from dropping open as the mother took out her list of grievances against me.

Among their list of my most irritating and unacceptable behaviors were

- I didn't inform them that some of the children were using thin crayons, and they had sent thick ones.

- I didn't notice their daughter wasn't drinking anything at lunch because she wasn't using her milk tickets.

- I didn't send home extensive art projects for her to complete at home when she was sick, and therefore she didn't have the same amount of artwork displayed as the other students.

There were other accusations questioning my teaching ability. My attempts to explain the reasoning behind decisions and actions were met by the parents with disbelief, disdain, and disgust. They had heard positive things about my classroom, and I had failed to meet their expectations. In no uncertain terms, I was informed they did not like me. While I'm sure these were not the first parents to dislike me, they were the first to boldly tell me.

(Continued)

(Continued)

I grew silent and slid my chair away from the group. I recall saying I was sorry that my actions had been misinterpreted and therefore offensive to them. I assured them I loved their child and would continue to teach her to the best of my ability. My principal thanked them for coming and announced that our meeting was over. She left them with the thought that perhaps our (private) school wasn't a good fit for their child if they didn't trust my judgement or her support of my classroom policies and procedures. I was grateful for the defense of a wise administrator.

What did Cindy learn from this experience?

Upset and confused, I continued to talk with my principal after the parents left. She encouraged me to rise above the unfounded accusations and be as welcoming as possible despite their disdain for me. She encouraged me to call them, thank them for coming in and reassure them they would be welcome in my classroom at the Thanksgiving Tea held for parents later that week.

Reluctantly I called. The mother's voice gave away her surprise at hearing mine. I stated that despite the fact our meeting probably hadn't gone the way either of us hoped, they were welcome in my classroom any time and I looked forward to seeing them at the Thanksgiving Tea.

That small gesture must have spoken volumes to them, as they both came to the tea without creating any unnecessary tension in our room. My mother died the following month, and this mom took up a collection among the parents to send me a plant. The rest of the year went by without further incident or complaint.

I learned that parents' anger likely may be misplaced, and you do not have to own it. You can, however, acknowledge their feelings and give them time to express the hurt that may be behind the anger. Set aside your own hurt and disappointment, recognize the pride in your initial defensiveness, and attempt to appreciate another perspective. I also came to understand that parents have a unique perspective that needs to be valued and acknowledged. Parents of only children have more time and energy to invest in a student than those of multiple children. This sometimes comes with a skewed perspective and scrutiny of procedures. Acknowledge their love for their child, and then affirm your care and concern. These words and actions will go a long way to laying a foundation for future relationship building. Do everything you can to build a bridge of communication.

FIGURING OUT WHAT WORKS FOR YOU WHEN DEALING WITH DIFFICULT PARENTS: JOELLE WRIGHT

With time and experience, I have built confidence in myself and my teaching practices. Most angry parents are upset because they don't fully understand the situation. Good communication (and timely responses) can put out a fire before things escalate. Acknowledging the parent's feelings, validating them, reassuring them that you care about their child, acknowledging the talents/abilities of that child, and then explaining what happened or why you made the decision you did can calm a parent down. They react strongly out of fear, out of confusion, and sometimes because they are just angry at the world and you are an easy target. However, you are the professional. As a teacher, your job is to be the cool, calm, collected person who does everything they can to help your students. When parents know from the outset that you care about your students, and that you work very hard to see and meet their needs, they are far more likely to cut you some slack.

For example, if I have a student with ADHD-type behaviors who constantly needs to move and frequently acts impulsively, I can show that student, as well as his parents, that I see his needs. I acknowledge his needs, but I don't fault him for them. Instead, I give him an exercise ball to sit on, an elastic band around the legs of his desk, a fidget for his hands, and allow him to have opportunities for movement. This lets him know that I see him, and I want to help him. Then, when he acts impulsively, I can have an honest conversation about how we all make mistakes, but when we do, we acknowledge them, and we make things right. When parents see that I am doing all that I can to meet the needs of their child, they are not as likely to be upset with me during tense discussions about their child's behavior.

HOW TO WIN THE PERENNIAL HOMEWORK BATTLE: JOELLE WRIGHT

The homework plan I recommend might be more extreme than some teachers are willing to consider, but I honestly think that I gain more support and cooperation from

(Continued)

(Continued)

parents when I win the support of parents by not giving any homework in my classroom. Yes, students are still expected to read every night, but there are no more complicated homework assignments. I have read numerous research articles about how homework at the elementary level is ineffective and not beneficial to our students. They already have to work so hard during the school day. My promise to parents and students is that if my students work hard and give me their best effort during the school day, then they can have a much-deserved break once school gets out. This is honestly a huge relief and burden lifted from the shoulders of parents.

As a parent, I worked hard with my two daughters on homework. Even as a competent and capable teacher, I struggled to work with my younger daughter on homework, because she had worked so hard to use her brain during the day. Her brain was incapable of working on homework in the evening, regulating her emotions and holding herself together. She was in foster care before I adopted her, and part of her story is that she missed some of her foundational years of elementary school. Having academic struggles made learning hard for her, in addition to all of the other struggles she was managing. She kept herself composed all throughout the school day and worked so hard to learn and listen to her teacher. Her brain deserved a rest in the evening. Once I made the decision to eliminate homework in my classroom, it was like an instant buy-in from parents. They so appreciated this and felt validated as parents who work hard and just want family time with their children.

What did Joelle learn from this experience?

Since I decided to eliminate homework, I have barely had any angry parents in recent years. It has been liberating. Anyone who works with me knows that I also hold my students to really high expectations, and we work nonstop to succeed as a class. My students have rewarded their parents, themselves, and me with test scores that have given our school awards. My lack of homework assignments is in no way an indicator of lax expectations.

DEALING WITH PARENTS WHO WANT YOU TO BEND THE RULES: KATHY HOEDEMAN

My "most difficult" parent grows out of my position as a math resource teacher providing services to students who excel in math. The hardest individuals to deal with are those who think their child should be accelerated in math and join one of my classes to learn math a year or even two years ahead of their grade level. Though our district has a structured system in place for these students to be identified and placed in these classes—a system designed to meet a "demonstrated need"—parents often want to circumvent the system. They go to great lengths to put their kids through boot camp so they can test into the program, and when [the kids] don't qualify, [the parents] are angry with me (even though I am not the "gatekeeper"). Typically, these parents are very well educated, articulate, and strong willed, and definitely are advocating for their child with great feeling. The thing that makes this so hard for me to deal with is the fact that listening and responding to them requires that I collect data (hard and soft) that shows that their child, as wonderful as he or she might be, is not what this parent wants them to be. I hate it.

Right now, I am in the middle of a battle between a parent and our district that involves a student who *is* in my math class but is not identified as "gifted" according to the [state] standards or those of our district. The parent is fighting madly to change this, getting evaluations done by outside sources and going to great lengths to make this happen. I will soon be asked to complete our district's referral form, all of which is open to the parent, and I know she will not be happy with my honest observations. Having to prove to a parent that their delightful, above-average child is *not* highly gifted in mathematics is a challenge.

What has Kathy learned from this experience?

Kathy has learned she must stay neutral and deflect the anger and passion these parents feel. She has also learned that data is key to keeping parents focused on the realities of their child's abilities.

Nothing in my life, not religion or politics or even family of origin, has ignited in me more fierce determination, courage, or empowerment than becoming a parent. The love, the protective care, the commitment to doing what I thought was right for my kids gave this rather timid person a voice that was sometimes surprising. I remember that when I deal with parents. Sure, not all of them may be speaking or acting out of the best intentions, but it is helpful to consider they are speaking for their child—no wonder they are emotional. Perhaps I can give them a break and be the calm one here.

DEALING WITH PARENTS WHO HAVE TAKEN IN A CHILD FROM TRAUMA: JOELLE WRIGHT

Joelle Wright specializes in working with parents who have taken in a child from trauma. She suggests the following for teachers who feel challenged by such children.

If you are working with a parent who has taken in a child from trauma, take some time to recognize that there is more going on at home than you see in the classroom. That student might struggle in class, but they struggle 10 times more in the safety of their own homes. They have held it together all day long in class, but once at home they can have meltdowns, food issues, sleep issues, and bathroom issues. Kids are constantly fighting for control, and the only things they really can control are what they eat, where and how they sleep, and their toileting habits. That means they wet the bed, are constipated, have irregular sleep schedules, and might need food to feel secure, or refuse food for other reasons.

As the teacher, our job is to have insight and empathy into what our students are experiencing, and also what the parents are enduring. We need to realize when we assign big projects at home, or if we don't communicate with parents in a timely manner, their job becomes twice as hard. If we have an autistic student who loves schedules and routines, and we haven't given parents proper notice about a big change in an upcoming schedule, then we hold some responsibility and need to acknowledge that we have made that parent's job harder.

What did Joelle learn from this experience?

I have learned to be far more empathetic for parents who are dealing with difficult behavioral issues at home.

DEALING WITH A PARENT WHO WANTS TO MICROMANAGE YOUR INSTRUCTION: TAMI LIEBETRAU SMITH

After 18 years of teaching, I transferred from teaching second grade to kindergarten. The year has been one of the most difficult years with parents. I reached out to a parent whose daughter has been quite physically aggressive with other students in the class. The parent wanted to send her mom, who was a former teacher, to observe how they could best support the little girl. After the observation, the mom sent a letter to my principal and me making all sorts of demands regarding how to manage her daughter as well as everyone else in the class. She also gave me "suggestions" on how to improve my instruction.

I was appalled at the letter, as both my principal and I felt the visit to observe was more about judging me as a teacher than offering ways to support the child. I didn't follow my own advice of staying calm, and I let the letter affect me negatively. Thankfully, I have a principal who supports me, and she dealt with this situation as well as with the parent. However, the relationship had been damaged, and future communication was avoided on her part even though I still reached out at times. She didn't come for the scheduled parent conference, and it wasn't until the kindergarten music program recently that we actually spoke face to face. I could tell she was uncomfortable, but as soon as I complimented her daughter's amazing artwork, I could tell her face softened and she relaxed a little.

What did Tami learn from this experience?

Try not to take parents' negativity or backlash personally. Their behavior usually means they are unhappy with life or are dealing with an overload of stress, and some people take it out on others. Unfortunately, we teachers will often get the brunt of someone else's reactions. Just remember to stay calm, upbeat, and positive, and remind them you want to work together as a team to best help their child. I also learned that a well-timed compliment can do much to defuse a parent with whom you've had an unpleasant encounter.

SUMMING UP AND LOOKING AHEAD

Hopefully you have been taking mental notes and have settled on the "big idea" of this chapter: The most important thing to do when you're recovering from a distressing parental encounter is to do some reflection about what you can learn from the experience. If you linger too long on the negative cloud hanging over your brain, you may well find yourself repeating this experience. Your goal is not to have another angry parent experience because you know where the conference went off the rails, and you are determined not to let that happen again. To quote Joelle Wright, "As a teacher, your job is to be the cool, calm, collected person who does everything you can to help your students."

Just ahead you will find a variety of ways that you can continue to grow and learn with the goal of putting your best self forward.

CHAPTER 6

PUTTING YOUR BEST SELF FORWARD

His legs are not matches, for he is still setting the best foot forward.

—Sir Thomas Overby (1613)

You likely have heard some version of the above epigraph from your parents or teachers, urging you to put your proverbial best foot forward prior to a critical competition or big test. However, when it comes to dealing with dysfunctional parents, putting your best foot forward won't take you over the finish line. The experienced teachers who contributed their stories in the previous chapter can still recount in excruciating detail their early encounters with angry parents. These attacks that upended their confidence and temporarily shattered their excitement and motivation about being a teacher often came out of nowhere, shocking and traumatic for the teachers in their level of hostility.

You may wonder if there is anything *you* can do to inoculate your confidence and self-worth as an educator against personal attacks from angry and dysfunctional parents. Here it is: *Put your best self forward.* You can nurture your best self in multiple ways. Some of the ways employ specific tools that will require you to learn and practice new approaches to communication. Other ways focus on becoming more self-reflective and willing to change your attitudes, priorities, and habits. These ways often require more maturity and patience.

The following tools and approaches will help you put your best self forward whenever you interact with parents—a best self that is able to set aside your personal biases and fear of the unknown, thereby enabling you to keep calm and hold your temper in the face of hostility and dysfunction. These are ten ways you can foster your best self and then put it forward as you deal with parents who are angry, troubled, afraid, or just plain "crazy." Accompanying each of the ways are references to books and sources that contain further information should you wish to delve more deeply into the topics. However, do not be overwhelmed by the sheer number of the tools. Instead, choose one or two that focus on your needs. Better yet, gather your teammates together and do some role-playing. One teacher can play the role of an upset parent, and another can practice using one of the tools.

1. Pay attention to your "emotional immune system."
2. Nurture your best self around a set of personal traits that signify character.
3. Use the ABC strategy that will enable you to affirm, bridge to, and communicate with dysfunctional parents.
4. Strive to be a teacher leader and role model for both your students and their parents.
5. When confronted with parent bullies, conduct an assertive intervention.
6. Listen, validate, respond.
7. When faced with an issue in which you are culpable, practice taking the A Train.
8. Deposit ample amounts of trust in the Relationship Trust and Savings Bank.
9. Strive to become an assertive and self-differentiated teacher.
10. Pay attention to your physical immune system.

PAY ATTENTION TO YOUR "EMOTIONAL IMMUNE SYSTEM"

Make no mistake about it, teaching the students of difficult and disengaged parents can take its toll on your emotional immune system (EIS). Contributing educator Tresa Watson let her hair down for me in a rare moment of discouragement:

For me, the most difficult thing to cope with has been when parents give lip-service to working with me, and then are seldom available to talk, or don't show up at conferences. When a plan is in place, but parents don't follow through on their part, whether it be signing a note, monitoring homework, or just staying in contact, I feel overwhelmed. How am I, by myself, for six hours a day, supposed to help this child grow and learn without parent support? How can I focus on a student's assets when I'm overwhelmed by his/her deficits?

Leslie Charles, author of *Why Is Everyone So Cranky?* (1999), offers some powerful advice for how to handle your *personal* crankiness, which can often seem inevitable in the face of the discouragement and despair you sometimes feel when confronted with an onslaught of dysfunctional parents. Charles posits the following hypothesis: *We all possess an internal protective mechanism that can safeguard us from cranky outbreaks that come our way.* She calls this protective mechanism the "emotional immune system" (1999, p. 22). Your EIS is different from your physical immune system, but when your EIS is neglected and abused, it can seriously interfere with or compromise your physical immune system. How can you take charge of those angry, cranky feelings? Charles suggests that you first determine the size of the issue with a problem parent that is facing you.

When you have an encounter with an angry, troubled, afraid, or wildly dysfunctional parent, first figure out the size of the problem:

- Is the parent problem a small, medium, or large annoyance?

- Is the parent problem a slightly unsettling one or is it downright dangerous?

- Is the conflict you are facing with a parent just a minor conflict, or does it fall into the mortal combat category? (adapted from Charles, 1999)

Once you have identified the size of the parent problem, Charles suggests that you ask yourself how you plan to respond to the problem:

- Will you choose to be mildly irritated or wildly upset?

- Will you blow this off or will you blow up instead?

- How long do you plan to stay upset and why?

Let's take a look at Tresa's problem: parents who are unavailable and unsupportive. You might even call them missing in action. Tresa is understandably angry and cranky about these disengaged and detached parents. Figure 6.1 teases out the layers of Tresa's problem using Charles's hypothesis. She definitely needs ideas and possible solutions, "supplements" that will boost her EIS.

FIGURE 6.1   How to Pay Attention to Your Emotional Immune System: Tresa Watson

How Tresa Is Feeling About the Disengaged Parents of Her Students	Discussion: Author's Perspective
"The most difficult thing for me to cope with has been when parents give lip-service to working with me, and then are seldom available to talk, or don't show up at conferences."	From my perspective this seems like a fairly small annoyance. However, from Tresa's point of view, when parents don't show up for conferences, it is a major concern. Her use of the term *cope* suggests that this state of affairs is like some real pain that she continually has to ignore, almost like a loose tooth that your tongue keeps going back to and wiggling around.
"When a plan is in place, but parents don't carry through on their part, whether it be signing a note, monitoring homework, or just staying in contact, I feel overwhelmed."	The words *feeling overwhelmed* suggest that Tresa is experiencing some long-term emotional wear and tear.
"How am I, by myself, for six hours a day, supposed to help this child grow and learn without parent support?"	Tresa is feeling very alone and is highly focused on the lack of support she is getting from parents. This is beginning to sound more and more like a very unsettling problem for Tresa. Is Tresa really alone? This problem sounds like Tresa needs a team to support her. I want to run through the halls of Tresa's school and knock on doors to find an older student buddy who can help a child with homework, or a parent volunteer who could come alongside the student to be a mentor. I want someone to do some testing for a student like this to see if there are support services that the student is eligible for.
"How can I focus on a student's assets when I'm overwhelmed by deficits?"	Who has the deficits here? The student? The parents? The teacher? Charles's final question for Tresa is this: How long do you plan to stay upset and why?

How Tresa Is Feeling About the Disengaged Parents of Her Students	Discussion: Author's Perspective
	Here's the advice Charles gives: The minute you realize you're on a negative track, picture yourself driving a car and coming up to a light that is changing to red. Slam on your brakes. Don't allow the negative thought to continue. Put a positive image in your head instead. In Tresa's case, she could think of the progress she has been able to facilitate for this child in spite of the child's "parent deficit." Perhaps there is a kind word Tresa could write or say to these disengaged parents that might catch them at a vulnerable moment and create a desire for them to communicate with Tresa. Maybe Tresa could focus first on building some kind of relationship, frail though it may be, that doesn't require them to be responsible for something they should have done. Clearly these parents don't have it all together. They need a kind word.

Source: Adapted by permission from material contributed by Tresa Watson

Reprinted from *How to Deal With Parents Who Are Angry, Troubled, Afraid, or Just Seem Crazy: Teachers' Guide* by Elaine K. McEwan-Adkins. Thousand Oaks, CA: Corwin, www.corwin.com. Reproduction authorized for educational use by educators, local school sites, and/or noncommercial or nonprofit entities that have purchased the book.

NURTURE YOUR BEST SELF AROUND A SET OF PERSONAL TRAITS THAT SIGNIFY CHARACTER

A second way to put your best self forward is to cultivate a unique set of personal traits that signify character (McEwan, 2006).

- **Trait 1: Mission-Driven and Passionate.** The effective teacher is mission-driven, feeling a "call" to teach as well as a passion to help students learn and grow. To be a passionate teacher is to be someone in love with a field of knowledge, deeply stirred by issues and ideas that challenge our world, drawn to the dilemmas and potentials of the young people who come into class each day—or captivated by all of these (Fried, 1995, p. 1).

- **Trait 2: Positive and Real.** The highly effective teacher is positive and real, demonstrating the qualities of caring, empathy, respect, and fairness in relationships with students, parents, and colleagues. "Good teaching cannot be reduced to technique; good teaching comes from the identity and integrity of the teacher" (Palmer, 1998, p. 10).

AFFIRM, BRIDGE, COMMUNICATE (ABC)

The idea that you as a teacher might actually become skilled at using a specific strategy to compel or persuade difficult and dysfunctional parents to understand and even support your side of a very contentious problem that involves their children may seem a reach too far for you. You may think of yourself solely as an educator rather than a psychotherapist, but in order to achieve your academic goals with students you may have to become more skilled than you currently are at building bridges with difficult parents. I first became acquainted with the ABC tool while reading *The Opposite of Hate: A Field Guide to Repairing Our Humanity* (Kohn, 2018). The author introduces this tool in the context of having difficult conversations with individuals with whom we have strong differences and possibly even heated or somewhat hateful arguments. Think Thanksgiving dinner discussing politics with your Uncle George. Some of your differences with parents may be political, cultural, religious, or racial. Or, they may be philosophical or educational. Whatever differences you have, strive to find common ground, identify a way to bridge those differences, and begin to communicate. You can sit at the opposite end of the table from Uncle George, but you cannot avoid affirming, bridging, and communicating with parents. Here are the steps:

- **Step A: Affirm.** What aspect of what a parent is saying could you agree with? Find a feeling with which you can agree, and affirm that feeling. You definitely need to be authentic in your agreement. Surely you can find one thing about which to agree. For example, as you talk with parents about their strong objections regarding the consequences meted out to their son when he used some very colorful profane language to describe one of his classmates, search for something in their tirade to affirm. They believe their brilliant son is just exercising his First Amendment rights and should not be punished for using that. You can certainly agree with the parents that these rights are very important in a democracy.

- **Step B: Bridge.** Think of this second step as the point at which you make some kind of connection with the parent. If you stumble into thinking that the "B" step is where you say the word "but," you will totally negate the positive feelings that may have flowed from any agreement in the first step. Yes, he broke the rules and he's required to take his punishment. The case is not closed here. To bridge the gap that still exists between you and the parents, say something that might surprise the parents, such as, "The good news about Joshua is that he is a great public speaker and really makes an impression on his classmates when he speaks." Hopefully you and the parents can chuckle over whether that's the kind of impression you would want such a handsome young man to make.

- **Step C: Convince.** This is the point in the conversation where you try to communicate with Joshua's parents that even though he is a fast talker and can fluently string swear words together, you would like to work with them to channel his creativity into using these talents in a positive way. Let Joshua's parents know that he could very well be a successful public speaker and debater, but in order to do that he will have to learn to follow the rules of the competition. One way to help Joshua do that is to help him take responsibility for following the class rules and accepting the consequences.

LEAD BY EXAMPLE

Highly effective teachers know how to provide the kind of leadership that brings parents into an active partnership with them (McEwan, 2002, pp. 41–42). As you consider the following examples of how outstanding teachers model leadership for parents, reflect on the advice our experienced teachers provided in Chapter 5 that illustrates some of these leadership examples. Choose one or more of these practices to strengthen your leadership with parents.

- Teachers can lead through affirmation by making positive phone calls and writing positive notes to parents about their children.

- Teachers can lead through collaboration by asking parents for observations on their children's homework activities (e.g., difficulties, limitations, what went well).

- Teachers can lead through invitation by asking parents to evaluate their teaching practices, the assignments they give to students, and their homework policies.

- Teachers can lead through communication by providing parents with a written general description of what will be covered during the school year and a brief explanation of why these activities are important.

- Teachers can lead through information by providing parents with an ongoing assignment calendar of the work that will be covered in class and why this work is important.

CONDUCT AN ASSERTIVE INTERVENTION

The assertive intervention is a communication tool based on the work of Susan Scott (2002). She calls her version of the intervention a "fierce conversation"; however, I coined the term "assertive intervention" to cast the conversation in a more professional light. Think of this tool as a way of "telling the truth in love." Only when teachers care for *and* about parents are they willing to go the extra mile to help parents to confront behaviors that are damaging to them and their children. "A good [teacher] will listen to [parents] without judgment, accept the intensity of [their] feelings, respect [their] pain, and express concern. A really good [teacher] will, in addition, help [parents] to see the situation in a new way" (Rosen, 1998, p. 167).

Telling the truth in love using an assertive intervention is a way of helping angry parents deal with underlying causes of their anger over which neither you nor the parent has control: (a) the world is not fair, (b) the world is full of imperfection, and (c) you can't give them what they want. Your goal is to help parents discover this truth, because some problems will only be solved when parents change *their* behavior.

An assertive intervention is a particular kind of confrontation. Although the definitions of the terms *confront* and *confrontation* include the concepts of defiance or antagonism, there is a third meaning that I prefer: *acknowledging and meeting a problem parent face-to-face with honesty, boldness, and confidence.* To confront a parent in the context of an assertive intervention means making that individual aware in a forthright way that you have observed his or her behavior or heard what the person has said. You are comfortable about defining it in detail, naming it for what it is, and discussing it in a calm and rational way. You communicate to the parent that you will not ignore further manifestations of the problem. Assertive interventions are never arrogant, hostile, or antagonistic. Rather, they are respectful, persistent, and consistent.

Contributing educator Nancy Adamson describes the following encounter with a parent that provides a perfect opportunity for her to conduct an assertive intervention. Here's how she describes her encounter:

> My first encounter with a parent who really got under my skin was in a tuition summer camp that our school sponsors every summer. It usually is a great way to get to know students and their parents in a less structured and more informal setting. The mother in question began bullying me in a somewhat passive-aggressive way. All summer long she continued to tell me that she didn't think I'd be a strong enough teacher for her son. She would laugh in a condescending way and demean

me by saying that I was too kind and soft-hearted. By the end of the summer, I decided to mention it to the principal. He decided to move the student into the other first-grade class. Then the war began. The mother requested a conference, and during the meeting she and her husband attacked me verbally. I told them that after a summer of constantly being told that I wouldn't be an adequate teacher for their son, I concluded that they obviously didn't want me to be their son's teacher. At that point the mother backed down and said she was only teasing me and that she was just joking. Her husband was seemingly unaware of any of her shenanigans and looked at her with disgust. I was crushed. I'll never forget the way they made me feel. It was a terrible year. Even though I didn't have any more contact with them, they would avoid me and talk about me behind my back to anyone that would listen. My principal made it worse when he said that I should have never let them talk to me that way. Apparently as they were leaving our initial meeting, they proceeded to brag to him how they had put me in my place.

If you're confused with exactly what was going on with these parents, think about how Nancy was feeling. After the summer of being bullied by the parent, she concluded that perhaps these parents did not want their child to be in her classroom. The principal erroneously jumped to that same conclusion and put the child's name on the other first-grade class list. A rational individual would assume that after getting what she seemingly wanted, the mother would be happy. Not so fast. This parent is enjoying her ability to drive Nancy "crazy" and is angry that her control of the situation has been snatched away from her. Not one aspect of this crazy scenario had anything to do with her son and what teacher might be best for him. It was all about her.

Not every teacher will have the misfortune to run into a spiteful, passive-aggressive bully like the mother Nancy describes. An individual like this can demoralize and destroy your confidence and definitely undermine your best self. Unfortunately, Nancy's principal did little to ameliorate the situation. In fact, I'm sorry to say he made the whole situation worse. But, that is a topic for another book. Let's take a look at how Nancy *might* have handled the situation once she got wind of all the gossip and untruths this parent was peddling. She needed to have an assertive intervention with this parent to confront her inappropriate behavior.

Susan Scott (2002) describes an encounter like these as "one in which we come out from behind ourselves into the conversation and make it real" (p. 7). Often when you have a situation where parents or their children continue to do and say inappropriate things, you set up a meeting with a game plan and good intentions, and then end up talking too much and saying all the wrong things. Sometimes you never get to the point or tell the truth, hoping to avoid offending the parent. Scott describes the avoidance of which we are all guilty in this way:

> When there is simply a whole lot of talking going on, conversations can be so empty of meaning they crackle. Memorable conversations include breathing space. Slow down the conversation so that insight can occur in the space between words and you can discover what the conversation really wants and needs to be about. (p. xiv)

Assertive interventions are rarely conducted during a first or second meeting with a dysfunctional parent. They are generally structured after you have listened, observed, and explored the situation from a variety of angles. Sometimes you discover that you are dealing with a highly dysfunctional parent who is quite adept at avoiding the real issues, thereby keeping *you* in a constant state of anxiety. It's time for an assertive intervention.

Don't rush into this encounter until you feel confident about every word you want to say; you want to be relaxed, confident, and avoid saying too much or becoming robotic. Figure 6.2 provides a template on which to draft your statements. After you have written a concise statement in response to each of the seven prompts, time the delivery of your presentation. Your statements when read aloud should take no more than 60 seconds. Rehearse your presentation until you can give it fluently and with confidence; practice in front of your mirror, if necessary, and pay attention to your body language. Make your statements with a calm but assertive manner—remember, being assertive is the opposite of being aggressive.

Figure 6.3 contains an assertive intervention script that Nancy might have used to confront the parent who was bullying her and then gossiping about it to anyone who would listen.

If you decide to use an assertive intervention with a dysfunctional parent, you will discover that if you can stand the wait, the final step will be worth it. Be sure to schedule enough time for this meeting so that you won't be antsy while you're waiting for a parent to respond. The secret to a successful assertive intervention is to sit expectantly but calmly looking at the person. Don't have a stare-down, but don't fill the silence and let the parent off the hook.

If the parent says, "I don't have anything to say about this problem right now," then you might say, "Well, if you *did* have something to say, what would it be?" If Mrs. Martin

FIGURE 6.2   Assertive Intervention Planning Form

Prompt	Statements to Be Presented
Name the behavior you want the parent to eliminate.	
Explicitly describe the behavior. Focus on what the parent is doing that most interferes with working collaboratively to bring out the best in the child. If you can't sum up the problem in one or two short statements, you are tackling too much at once.	
Provide one or two specific examples of the behavior that you or others have observed, making sure that they adequately illustrate the impact the behavior is having.	
Describe your personal feelings about what the parent is doing; for example, shocked, distressed, embarrassed, or disappointed.	
Clarify what is at stake for the parent if the behavior persists; for example, describe how it is affecting the parent's reputation in the school and community.	
Identify your contribution to the problem. For example, if the problem is a persistent one and to date you have avoided confronting the parent, express regret that you have not done so sooner, and offer a possible reason for the delay.	
Strongly state your sincere desire to resolve the issue with speed. Indicate your willingness to move forward together, and include your expressed belief that eliminating the behavior will be an advantage to the parent as well as to the school.	
Invite the parent to respond.	

FIGURE 6.3   Assertive Intervention Script

Prompt	Statements to Be Presented
Name the behavior you want the parent to eliminate.	Mrs. Martin, I want to talk with you about the unkind and untrue things you are saying about me as a result of our meeting over your son's transfer.
Explicitly describe the behavior. Focus on what the parent is doing that most interferes with working collaboratively to bring out the best in the child. If you can't sum up the problem in one or two short statements, you are tackling too much at once.	You are gossiping to others about me.
Provide one or two specific examples of the behavior that you or others have observed, making sure that they adequately illustrate the impact the behavior is having.	For example, yesterday you bragged to the principal and two teachers about exactly how you put me in my place.
Describe your personal feelings about what the parent is doing, for example, shocked, distressed, embarrassed, or disappointed.	I'm extremely disappointed in you and very distressed in how you are spreading rumors and gossiping about me.
Clarify what is at stake for the parent if the behavior persists; for example, describe how it is affecting the parent's reputation in the school and community.	Your behavior seriously damages your reputation as a caring parent in the eyes of other parents and faculty members and provides a poor role model for your son as well.
Identify your contribution to the problem. For example, if the problem is a persistent one and to date you have avoided confronting the parent, express regret that you have not done so sooner, and offer a possible reason for the delay.	I should have talked to you the first time somebody told me what you were saying about me, but I ignored the situation thinking you would realize how inappropriate it was.
Strongly state your sincere desire to resolve the issue with speed. Indicate your willingness to move forward together, and include your expressed belief that eliminating the behavior will be an advantage to the parent as well as to the school.	When you leave my classroom today, I would like to know that we won't ever have to have this discussion again.
Invite the parent to respond.	Tell me what you think is going on here.

still refuses to answer, you might say, "I have no idea what's going on here, Mrs. Martin, but I could make a good guess, if you won't talk to me about this problem."

At that point, you might venture a guess to Mrs. Martin about the reasons behind her behavior: "Maybe you hated school when you were a kid, and every time you walk through the school door you feel like you're back in elementary school, and you get so mad that you can't hold it in." If that doesn't register with Mrs. Martin, try this guess on for size: "Maybe I said something to you in the beginning of the year and you just can't stand me or the idea of your son being in my classroom, so every time you see me, you do something outrageous to see if maybe I'll get mad at you and you'll have an excuse to ask for your son's transfer out of my class."

At this point, Mrs. Martin may break down to tell you that she has been under a lot of stress lately since her husband is moving out and that she feels terrible about her behavior and is humiliated by her immaturity and poor judgment. Bingo. Now you and Mrs. Martin can move on to solve this problem. If Mrs. Martin is not willing to respond, your 60-second intervention might be all that is needed to put her on notice that you are aware of what she is doing and won't stand for it. Thank her for listening and remind her that you will be coming back to her again if you hear her talking about you and spreading gossip.

If the parent fails to acknowledge the existence of the behavior or seems unwilling at that time to do anything about it, your assertive intervention has not "failed." The parent just needs additional time and another intervention in order to realize two things: (1) You are serious in your intent to deal with the problem, and (2) there are benefits to be realized from making the change. You might even consider inviting your principal to your next assertive intervention. He doesn't have to say a word, but his presence will speak volumes.

Please note that assertive interventions can also work with troublesome colleagues who aren't pulling their weight on a team, nagging spouses who are causing you sleepless nights, and teenagers who need to know you're serious about curfews. The first time I used an assertive intervention was during my first year as a principal. My predecessor, who had left several messy personnel issues for me to clean up, had the nerve to gossip about me to some of his staff members who had joined him at the new school. I phoned him up and told him that I was sorry to hear about the untrue things he was spreading about me to his faculty. I suggested that if we were going to be colleagues on an administrative team, we would have to trust each other and that his behavior was untrustworthy. I suggested that this be the last time we talked about this issue, and amazingly enough we became good colleagues if not best buddies for the next eight years. That experience sold me on the power of assertive interventions.

Listen, Validate, Respond

In addition to using tools from published authors, don't overlook the possibility that you could develop a simple script that fits you and your communication style just perfectly. For example, here's a three-step process developed by contributing educator Joelle Wright.

When dealing with an angry parent, I use the following three steps: Listen, Validate, and Respond. Parents want to be heard—even if what they have to say doesn't apply to the situation at hand. Typically, if there is any miscommunication, I will often apologize quickly that I didn't let them know sooner, or explain a problem more fully. Even if there is nothing specific for me to apologize for, a brief and cursory apology can be quick and painless, and make a parent automatically feel better. I also try to find an opportunity to thank parents for something great they are doing with their child at home. This can be a chance to thank them for supporting their child's education, for helping the child to be successful in the classroom, or for caring enough to double-check about a miscommunication. If I can honestly say it, I will even be sure to tell a parent that their child is lucky to have someone who cares so much about him or her. Those personal steps of acknowledging and validating where the parent is coming from, how they are feeling, and how hard they work at home will go a long way toward building a positive relationship and diffusing a situation. Parents are always tired and overworked. They constantly doubt whether they are making the right choices. If you can make them feel better, feel heard, and feel reassured that their child is safe and well taken care of, then they are less likely to hold on to their anger.

Set up some easy communication tools. I always give a family survey at the beginning of the year in which parents can give a little background info about their child, family dynamics, et cetera. They can give demographic info, but then you ask them for insights into their child. This allows you to acknowledge that they are the experts and know what works best for their student. I also open up my classroom to volunteers. They might not be able to come in, but at least they know they are always welcome. Every parent who does stop by to volunteer offers me opportunities to constantly affirm and appreciate every little thing they do. Try to give affirmations to parents about the positive progress their children are making in addition to the less positive news you may have to deliver at times about your concerns.

TAKE THE A TRAIN

Highly critical parents often have only one mission in life: to find fault with something. It could be your grammar and spelling in the class newsletter, the way in which you have handled a discipline issue with their child, or the fact that you said something totally inappropriate. The problem is that these parents may be right on in their judgment about something you have done. I like the advice that Sam Horn (1996) gives in her book, *Tongue Fu!* She suggests taking the A Train to deal with hypercritical people.

Perhaps mention of the A Train stirs memories of your first subway ride in New York City, or, if you're fond of big band music, you might think immediately of Duke Ellington's classic. But for dealing with picky people, Horn suggests a different kind of A Train, one that takes you and a highly critical parent to a more productive relationship. Choose one or more of these four possibilities: (1) acknowledge, (2) agree, (3) apologize, or (4) appreciate. Here's how the A Train works. *Acknowledge* the existence of the problem to the critical parent, if indeed the problem is a real one. *Agree* that it is a worthy problem that needs a solution, if indeed it does. Don't be reluctant to *apologize* (either personally or corporately) for what did or didn't happen (if appropriate). And, if you are feeling particularly magnanimous, express your *appreciation* to the parent for bringing the problem to your attention, indicating that you will do all in your power to correct it.

Don't become defensive or accusatory. Of course, taking the A Train only works when picky parents identify real problems that *can* be solved. Parents who complain about things over which neither you nor they have any control (for example, the number of students who don't speak English, or the changing demographics of your school) have a different set of problems.

Contributing educator Kathy Hoedeman shares her experience with an angry parent that provided the perfect opportunity to use the A Train.

The quivering and quaking began when I answered the phone and the parent began talking. It continued into the meeting the next day. I was part of an innovative middle school team where two teachers, an intern, and two aides had responsibility for 80 students. I was new, the intern was assigned to the other teacher for the first nine weeks, and I was alone in a classroom with 40 sixth graders in a room designed for 30.

My previous experience had been with elementary students, and I had yet to develop my thick-skinned, tough-on-the-outside middle school persona. I cared, maybe way too much, about who was learning and who was not. I had a male student who was making every choice not to learn, consequently interrupting the learning of others, and breaking this soft, loving teacher's heart. It had to get to me—and it did.

At the key point in that day's math lesson, when he asked to leave the room, I was about at my breaking point. Knowing he would miss the essential learning, be unable to complete the formative assessment, get discouraged and give up, make a fuss at home about how he couldn't do the work, fail the test, never graduate from high school—I smiled and granted him permission to go to the bathroom.

Then I broke, and under my breath I made an inappropriate comment about choosing not to learn and the consequences being out of my control. Well, this student had a friend that told him I said something derogatory about him to the whole class (he may not have heard my exact words, but he certainly got the gist of them). He told his mom, and mom was really angry.

I quivered and quaked because I knew I was wrong. I did not try to defend myself on the phone, but asked her to call the office and schedule a conference (the procedure for all parent requested conferences in our building). Then, I immediately went to my principal and "confessed." I admitted that I was wrong. Yes, the child was a very difficult one. Yes, the family was not supporting learning at home. But, I was wrong. Fortunately, my principal was wise and said he would meet with us, though as an observer. He counseled me to describe as objectively as I could what had happened and admit that I had been in the wrong. Then we would see where the conversation took us.

I remember my principal asking the mom to express her concerns to start. We just let her speak, no interruptions, questions, or defensive statements. Then he invited me to share. It was a long time ago and I don't remember the exact words that were spoken, but I do remember that my admission of guilt and a promise to treat her child with the respect that was due him, and every child in my classroom, ended the issue.

DEPOSIT TRUST IN YOUR RELATIONSHIP TRUST AND SAVINGS BANK

The term *relational capital* has its origin in the business world and is thought of as "a type of intangible value established by a business based on its reputation and relationships with stakeholders" (Spacey, 2017). Teacher Stacey May describes it this way in the context of building relationships with parents:

> Relationships [with parents] need to be invested in and developed. That takes time, effort and empathy. Ensure that you make positive connections with as many of the parents of your students as you can. When you catch your students doing great stuff, write home about it. This way you have built rapport and relational capital with the parents. Then, if you have to speak with them about something that's not so great, you have already formed a relationship with the parent and have relational capital that you can draw on.

Parents can only care for you when they know you care about them and theirs. If this kind of caring and empathy is provided to parents over time, you can later "cash in" on some of that relationship investment when it comes to reaching understanding and buy-in from difficult parents. Similarly, you can't walk into a bank without having deposited money and expect to withdraw money or claim you have a stake in the business relationship. We can't expect parents to entrust their children to us as teachers unless we have built or are building one of the most important aspects of relational capital: *relational trust.* In their research on improving low-performing schools, Bryk and Schneider (2002) found that relational trust generates a moral imperative to take on the hard work of school improvement (pp. 122–123). It can also generate a willingness in parents to work together with you to join with you in helping their students achieve academic success.

Relational trust as described and measured by Bryk and Schneider (2002) is a construct composed of four concepts: (1) respect, (2) competence, (3) personal regard, and (4) integrity (McEwan, 2009, pp. 79–81).

Respect

Respect is the deference someone shows to others without regard for their political position, wealth, job role, or power. Parents are assumed to love their children and to be doing the best they know how to do for them, until there is solid evidence to the contrary. Therefore, even when parents do not get what they want (a new teacher for their child, forgiveness of an after-school detention, or a change of a report card grade), they will feel as though their opinions were recognized as valid and that they were treated with fairness. Parents are highly sensitive to microinequities, subtle slights of verbal and nonverbal communication that result from an imbalance of power between two people such as parent and teacher (Rowe, 1990). Examples of microinequities include fidgeting, not maintaining eye contact, looking right through someone, interrupting, furrowing one's brow, and ignoring what someone has said.

Competence

Competence is the ability to do something in a superior way, for example, the ability to teach previously low-achieving students and bring them to mastery, or the ability to motivate and instill a love of learning in students. Parents want their children to do well in school, and they desire the very best teachers.

Personal Regard

Personal regard is the presence of positive feelings toward someone. When individuals like each other, they enjoy being together. However, personal regard goes beyond just liking people. It includes a willingness to extend or even inconvenience oneself. For example, in the case of teachers, if they have high regard for parents, they will be inclined to stay late for a quick parent conference, tutor children during a free period, or make phone calls to parents from their homes in the evening.

Integrity

Integrity refers to an individual's adherence to certain moral principles and standards. Integrity also speaks to a level of consistency and reliability in people's behavior. When they promise they will do something, they follow through. Individuals with integrity are often described as having character.

Consider how trust can be undermined or even destroyed in just one aspect of school life—the chain of events that can rapidly unfold when the members of the school community do not trust each other to do their jobs. They do not trust the competence of other members of the community. If parents and teachers do not trust one another to fulfill their role obligations, there is a strong likelihood that everyone will suffer, but most of all the students. For example, if teachers don't believe that students are competent to achieve the grade-level standards, their low expectations create a trust issue that in turn further depresses achievement. Parents who don't feel that the teachers in a school are competent to teach their children become distrustful, and in turn communicate this distrust to their offspring, who in turn become discipline problems. Teachers who believe that parents aren't competent to parent their offspring, and communicate this lack of trust in both spoken and unspoken ways, create angry and hostile parents.

A high level of relational trust between and among parents, students, and teachers is essential to achieving any one of many compelling missions you might choose to achieve in your classroom. Relational trust impacts student motivation and engagement that are in turn positively associated with increased achievement and appropriate behavior in your classroom.

Contributing educator Susan Burke explains how critical this aspect of trust-building can be:

> The parents who need an extra measure of empathy and understanding as you attempt to gain their trust are those who personally have had frustrating or downright traumatic experience with an educational system. I try to gain their trust very quickly and let them know I am there to help them in any way I can. Creating a safe place for parents to ask questions and get help is the first step in gaining the buy-in I need from them to keep them excited about their child's success in school. At our family conference in the fall, I start to build that relationship and invite the parent to be a part of the school family. I have an open door to volunteers and provide any opportunity for the parent to be a part of our daily routines, including family homework commitments. The system can be overwhelming and intimidating. I offer support in all areas. I answer questions about IEPs, act as a liaison with special services, offer to follow them to the next grade, and navigate what seems to be an overwhelming experience. This process requires that I acquire as much knowledge as I can about the support services available in the school and community.

BECOME AN ASSERTIVE AND SELF-DIFFERENTIATED TEACHER

Self-differentiation is your ability to maintain boundaries between yourself and parents. Being best friends with the parents of your students is asking for relationship difficulties. A self-differentiated individual, who feels confident and worthwhile, is able to put the words and deeds of angry parents in perspective. Assertive teachers are (a) mature and self-defined, (b) unwilling to take personal responsibility for the difficulties of dysfunctional parents, and (c) not readily distracted from the goals of the stated academic vision and mission by parents' inappropriate behaviors. Here are the capacities of self-differentiated teachers that set them apart:

- The capacity to view oneself separately from parents with a minimum amount of anxiety (worry or fear) or polarization (extreme identification with) to the positions (responses, behavior, attitudes) or reactivity (anger, anxiety, exhaustion, or confusion) of parents

- The ability to maintain a nonanxious presence (i.e., an attitude, stance, or frame of mind in which an individual can be present and attuned to what is happening now without worrying about tomorrow) when working with and interacting with parents who are angry, troubled, afraid, or totally dysfunctional

- The maturity to chart one's own course by means of an internal guidance system (i.e., a set of personal values) rather than continually trying to figure out what others are thinking (i.e., seeing which way "the wind is blowing")

- The wisdom to be clear and committed about one's personal values and goals

- The willingness to take responsibility for one's own emotional being and destiny rather than blaming either others or uncontrollable cultural, gender, or environmental variables (adapted from Friedman, 1991, pp. 134–170)

Learning to put your best self forward is a maturation process, but one worthy of self-examination and assessment.

Dysfunctional parents often want you to do their homework for them. Let me explain. As the team leader and department chair, Sandy is often asked to meet with parents who are unhappy with some aspect of instruction or assessment. For example, she might meet with the parents of a child who got a low grade that will impact his transcript for college entrance; a teacher in her department has said something inappropriate to this child. They want Sandy to solve this problem—to magically wave her wand, change the report card grade on the transcript, and improve the teacher's relationship with their child. Of course, they want all of this to happen, but they don't want the teacher to know for fear he will take it out on their son. This is a perfect example of triangulation. The parents are unwilling to sit down with the teacher and are afraid of confronting him, and they want Sandy to solve the problem for them.

Sandy's first question for the parents should be, "Have you talked to the teacher about this?" If their answer is "No," then she should send them straight to the source of their irritation. Beware of being triangulated—caught between two (or more) people who should be talking to each other, but instead are attempting to put you in charge of their problems. The teacher needs to communicate with the parents directly and explain the reasons for the low grade and the "back story" of the "words" exchanged between him and his student. If the department chair is in charge of the teacher's evaluation, then she may have some responsibilities with regard to his performance. If she is not, then she is not in charge of solving this problem. Learning to say no is part of being a self-differentiated individual.

Figure 6.4 displays the Assertive Teacher Self-Assessment. As you seek to put your best self forward, periodically assess your progress toward becoming an assertive and self-differentiated individual who is continually managing your best self.

FIGURE 6.4   The Assertive Teacher Self-Assessment

	Never	Seldom	Sometimes	Usually	Always
Indicator 1	1	2	3	4	5
I protect and honor my own rights as an individual as well as the rights of parents and students.					
Indicator 2	1	2	3	4	5
I recognize the importance of boundaries and am able to stay connected to others while at the same time maintaining a sense of self and individuality.					
Indicator 3	1	2	3	4	5
I have positive feelings regarding myself and am thus able to create positive feelings on the part of students and parents.					
Indicator 4	1	2	3	4	5
I am willing to take risks, but I recognize that mistakes and failures are part of the learning process.					
Indicator 5	1	2	3	4	5
I am able to acknowledge and learn from my successes as well as my failures.					
Indicator 6	1	2	3	4	5
I am able both to give compliments and receive constructive criticism from parents and students.					

(Continued)

FIGURE 6.4   (Continued)

	Never	Seldom	Sometimes	Usually	Always
Indicator 7	1	2	3	4	5
I make realistic promises and commitments to parents and am able to keep them.					
Indicator 8	1	2	3	4	5
I genuinely respect the ideas and feelings of parents and students.					
Indicator 9	1	2	3	4	5
I am willing to compromise and negotiate with parents in good faith.					
Indicator 10	1	2	3	4	5
I am capable of saying no to parents and sticking to a position, but I do not need to have my own way at all costs.					
Indicator 11	1	2	3	4	5
I can handle anger, hostility, put-downs, and lies from parents without undue distress, recognizing that I am defined from within.					
Indicator 12	1	2	3	4	5
I can handle anger, hostility, put-downs, and lies from parents without responding in kind.					
Indicator 13	1	2	3	4	5
I am aware of my personal emotions (e.g., anger, anxiety), can name them, and can manage them.					
Indicator 14	1	2	3	4	5
I am prepared for and can cope with the pain that is a normal part of being a classroom teacher.					

TEND TO YOUR HEALTH

At the beginning of this chapter, we discussed the importance of tending to your EIS in order to be prepared for whatever the next encounter with an angry and dysfunctional parent might bring to your classroom door. Neglecting your physical health can also leave you unprepared for assaults from angry parents. That wise guru Leslie Charles recommends tending to your health with these six simple questions. Failing to answer just one or two in the favor of good health can leave you putting the "wrong foot forward" when it comes to dealing with challenging students and dysfunctional parents. Pick just one of these key areas to work on.

- Are you continually rushed and pressed for time?
- When was the last time you did anything for fun or had time for relaxation?
- Are you neglecting your health in any way?
- Do you constantly feel worried and apprehensive?
- Is there a relationship in your life that needs attention?
- Are you working more and enjoying it less? (Charles, 1999)

ONE AT A TIME OR ALL AT ONCE

There are two ways to process the information, advice, and strategies found in this book. You can think of the book as a smorgasbord of wonderful options and choose one or two of the most applicable pieces of information to focus on for a time, and then go back for more as the need to become more skilled arises.

Or, you can decide you want to digest the whole enchilada in one bite and become an expert on parental communication overnight. The second approach will likely leave you seriously sleep deprived and with an accompanying headache and upset tummy.

Here's one option for assimilating this material in a seamless and painless way. Take some time in your grade-level team meetings to do some role-playing, with one set of team members playing the roles of dysfunctional parents, another set of teachers sharing how they will respond to these "angry parents," and a third set of team members critiquing and discussing how skillfully the "teachers" dealt with the "dysfunctional parents." You will not become skilled at dealing with dysfunctional parents overnight, but over time you will be amazed at how easily you managed to defuse and disarm a parent without even breaking a sweat or shedding a tear.

Be sure to take time to process the conclusion just ahead. It offers you 10 goals to keep you on track to becoming a communication guru.

CONCLUSION

10 Goals to Help You Deal With Difficult Parents

To be aware of a single shortcoming within oneself is more useful than to be aware of a thousand in somebody else.

—The Dalai Lama (n.d.)

There are multiple agendas competing for the attention of today's teachers. I submit, however, that the 10 goals described in this conclusion are more important than anything else currently on your to-do list. You may think that your highest priority at the moment is having all of your students score a "proficient" rating on state assessments, but allow me to suggest that all of your detailed improvement plans to will fail if you do not bring all of the parents in your classroom community alongside your efforts—especially the ones who are currently stirred up like a hornet's nest.

In all likelihood, a fair number of these upset parents have children who aren't doing well in school. You need their unqualified support to bring their children up to grade level. A significant number of angry parents have children who *are* doing well, but these parents are dismayed because the behavioral and academic standards in your school don't quite meet their expectations. They are considering home schooling, private school options, or perhaps a charter school. For your school to be their school of choice, you need to find out what's troubling them, and if possible, fix it. A mass exodus of students from your attendance area could leave you looking for another job. Here then are the 10 goals on which to focus in the weeks ahead.

1. Give parents what they want.

You no doubt cringed when you read this first goal: *Give parents what they want.* You may be thinking that I have taken leave of my senses. However, consider what it is that parents really do want:

- Effective teachers for their children
- Achievement by their children
- Communication from the teacher
- Safety and discipline in the classroom and on the playground
- Opportunities for meaningful involvement

If you give parents what they want, you will wake up one sunny school morning as the teacher of the year. Parents crave teachers who are effective—individuals who have personal traits that signify character, teaching traits that get results, and intellectual traits that demonstrate knowledge, curiosity, and awareness (McEwan, 2002).

Parents want their children to learn and achieve in school. Some parents have expectations that their children will attend highly competitive universities, but most parents just want their children to know and be able to do more this year than they could last year. They want them to learn to read, write, and compute; have some knowledge of history and science; and if they're really fortunate, learn a foreign language. When students spend days and years and get a diploma from high school without knowing how to read and write, parents get understandably upset.

Parents crave communication—not just newsletters that recycle the same tired information, platitudes, and admonitions, but real communication that specifically describes how their children are doing, tells them what's going on at school, and gives them practical and reasonable ways they can help their children at home.

Parents want, deserve, and must have safety and discipline in the classrooms their children attend. Parents never fully trust teachers who aren't constantly about the business of making sure that the school grounds, hallways, and classrooms are physically and emotionally safe for all children. Educators who are unable to work together to create a warm, inviting, and secure school community are suspect in parents' eyes.

Last, parents want to be involved. They want involvement that goes beyond fundraisers and booster clubs. They want the kind of involvement that ensures that their voices will be heard, their needs will be considered, and their importance will be valued, even when they make mistakes, get angry, and lose their tempers occasionally.

If you give parents these five "intangibles," they will picket when the school board wants to close your school, lobby for a raise for you at the next school board meeting, and request you as the teacher for every child in their family that will soon be enrolling in your school.

2. Be proactive rather than reactive.

No doubt you have already carefully read Chapter 5, absorbing the advice of teachers regarding what proactive steps they recommend you take at the beginning of every school year. Their suggestions will help you to build trust, establish positive communication with the new crop of parents, and enable you to hit the ground running with your goals for the school year. The more proactive steps you can successfully implement, the fewer angry parents you will have knocking on your classroom door.

3. Build relationships.

Relationship building with parents is done one parent at a time. Here are some ways to do it:

- Determine parents' interests and strengths. Assess the talents of parents who may be able to speak to your class or teach an enrichment class in some aspect of art or science, or help students paint a mural on the wall of your literacy corner.
- Give parents advance warning. Everything that happens at school is of interest to parents. Don't make the mistake of thinking you can ask parents for forgiveness instead of telling them up front what you have planned.

4. Tend to teaching.

Your most important responsibility as a teacher is to teach with passion and effectiveness, in order that your students will be successful in your classroom. As part of the back-to-school meeting you have with parents, remind them of your expectations of them with regard to their children. Then assure them that you will do your very best to teach every child to master the expected outcomes of your grade level. Let them know that you will never blame them when their children don't learn or behave.

Tell them things such as the following: My doors will always be open to you. To make you feel welcome, I will always have two adult-sized chairs just inside my door expressly for parents to sit in. You do not need to make a special appointment to visit my classroom. You just need stop in the office and make your presence known, sign in, receive a guest badge, and then follow the school rules. (Parents who do not follow the rules will be asked to leave the building. Deal with them immediately.) I promise that to the best of my ability I will not send homework assignments home with your students that they are not able to complete independently. I will try my hardest to have already conducted an "I do it; we do it; you do it; apply it" teaching sequence.

5. Don't hit your ball into the seven sand traps.

Perhaps you don't play golf or even watch golf tournaments on television. If not, let me explain what a sand trap is. It is a spot on the golf course that is designed to make the game more challenging. Sand traps slow down your game, decrease the likelihood that you will come out a winner, and use up energy that could be devoted to more productive moves. The seven sand traps listed here can lessen your effectiveness during your encounters with angry parents. Avoid them at all costs:

- The trap of talking too much or too fast
- The trap of interrupting or not listening
- The trap of becoming angry at the angry parent
- The trap of refusing to apologize when you know you should
- The trap of using too much jargon and too many big words
- The trap of getting caught in a power struggle
- The trap of changing the rules or applying them to suit the situation, even if it gives the angry parents what they want

6. Deal with yourself.

If you desire to be the kind of teacher about whom parents say, "You can always go to him with a problem," or "She is always looking out for the kids," or "He is a straight-shooter," or "You can trust her," then you must learn to manage your own emotions, behaviors, and attitudes. You must determine where your "hot buttons" are and then diligently work to make sure that no one else ever discovers them.

7. Build a well-balanced team.

When teachers work as a team, there will be far fewer angry parents. If the secretarial staff, teaching staff, health office personnel, bus drivers, custodians, and cafeteria workers *all* know what the culture of the school demands of them with regard to their treatment of parents and students, your life will be a bed of roses, so to speak. Well, there may be a few thorns here and there, but there will be far fewer than if team members do and say just what they feel like doing in any given circumstance.

8. Don't drive parents crazy!

After years of writing newspaper columns and being on talk radio shows, I am certain that in some schools, staff members go out of their way to drive parents crazy. They seem to specialize in doing the following:

- Not returning telephone calls
- Telling parents to trust them and then abusing that trust
- Stonewalling and circling the wagons to protect inappropriate behavior on the part of fellow staff members
- Stereotyping and treating parents prejudicially
- Acting arrogantly
- Using educational jargon to confuse simple issues
- Defending people who are incompetent
- Lying to parents

9. Tell the truth in love.

We have an obligation as educators to help parents become better and to help children who are not succeeding. Often that means confronting difficult issues and telling parents that unless we all change what we are doing, their children are on a collision course with serious problems down the road. This is never easy, but you never want to hear parents say: "Why didn't you tell me that a long time ago?" and not have an answer like, "Remember when we had that meeting at the beginning of the school year and we talked about the importance of being on the same page with regard to Matt's lack of responsibility?"

10. Address small problems before they get bigger.

There *are* rare instances when what appears to be a huge problem resolves itself without intervention. But putting your head in the sand like the proverbial ostrich is generally a recipe for disaster. Hoping that the playground bully will miraculously see the error of his ways just won't work. Smoking in the girls' bathrooms will not disappear on its own but will likely spawn an epidemic of graffiti. Addressing small problems before they become major ones is essential in schools. Frequently, a minor problem, if ignored, can become an article in the newspaper, a lawsuit at the courthouse, a picket line in front of your school, or the loss of your job.

I hope that you now feel more confident regarding your ability to deal with difficult parents. Building relationships with parents toward the goal of helping all students grow intellectually, socially, and academically is not only in our job description. One of my favorite research studies is titled *Kids Don't Learn From Teachers They Don't Like* (Aspley, 1979). A corollary study might well test this hypothesis: *Kids don't learn when their parents and the teacher don't get along.*

REFERENCES

Argyris, C. (1986). Skilled incompetence. *Harvard Business Review, 64*, 74–79.

Argyris, C. (1991). Teaching smart people how to learn. *Harvard Business Review, 69*, 99–109.

Aspley, G. (1979). *Kids don't learn from teachers they don't like*. London: Academic Press.

Autry, J. A. (2001). *The servant leader: How to build a creative team, develop great morale, and improve bottom-line performance*. Roseville, CA: Prima.

Axelrod, A., & Holtje, J. (1997). *201 ways to deal with difficult people*. New York: McGraw-Hill.

Bailey, S. (1971). Preparing administrators for conflict resolution. *Educational Record, 53*, 225.

Brinkman, R., & Kirschner, R. (1994). *Dealing with people you can't stand*. New York: McGraw-Hill.

Brody Communications Ltd. (2004). *Strengthening interpersonal relationships*. Retrieved November 12, 2018, from http://www.brodycommunications.com

Bryk, A. S., & Schneider, B. (2002). *Trust in schools: A core resource for improvement*. New York: Russell Sage Foundation.

Charles, C. L. (1999). *Why is everyone so cranky?* New York: Hyperion.

Covey, S. (n.d.). BrainyQuote.com. Retrieved December 23, 2018, from BrainyQuote.com

Covey, S. R. (1989). *7 habits of highly effective people*. New York: Simon & Schuster.

Covey, S. R. (1998). Growing great children. In M. S. Josephson & W. Hanson (Eds.), *The power of character: Prominent Americans talk about life, family, work, values, and more* (pp. 99–106). San Francisco: Jossey-Bass.

Crowe, S. (1999). *Since strangling isn't an option: Dealing with difficult people—common problems and uncommon solutions*. New York: Perigee.

Drucker, P. (n.d.). BrainyQuote.com. Retrieved November 6, 2018, from http://www.brainyquote.com.

Dulles, J. F. (n.d.). BrainyQuote.com. Retrieved November 6, 2018, from http://www.brainyquote.com

Einstein, A. (n.d.). On the formulation of a problem by Albert Einstein. Retrieved November 6, 2018, from http://www.gurteen.com/gurteen/gurteen.nsf/id/X00001A96/

Fried, R. I. (1995). *The passionate teacher: A practical guide.* Boston: Beacon Press.

Friedman, E. H. (1991). Bowen theory and therapy. In A. S. Gurman & D. P. Kniskern (Eds.), *Handbook of family therapy* (pp. 134–170). New York: Brunner/Mazel.

Hamachek, D. (1999). Effective teachers: What they do, how they do it, and the importance of self-knowledge. In R. P. Lipka & T. M. Brinthaupt (Eds.), *The role of self in teacher development* (pp. 189–224). Albany: State University of New York Press.

Heasley, S. (2018, June 5). *Special education enrollment trends upward.* Retrieved December 24, 2018, from disabilityscoop.com.

Horn, S. (1996). *Tongue fu! How to deflect, disarm, and defuse any verbal conflict.* New York: St. Martin's Griffin.

Kipling, R. (1936). If. In H. Felleman (Ed.), *The best loved poems of the American people* (p. 65). Garden City, NY: Doubleday.

Kohn, S. (2018). *The opposite of hate: A field guide to repairing our humanity.* Chapel Hill, NC: Algonquin Books of Chapel Hill.

Kottler, J. A., & McEwan, E. K. (1999). *Counseling tips for elementary school principals.* Thousand Oaks, CA: Corwin.

Lao-Tzu. (1992). *Tao te ching: A new English version.* Foreword and notes by Stephen Mitchell. New York: Harper Perennial. (Original version from the 6th c. BCE)

Lemov, D. (2014). *Teach like a champion. 2.0.* San Francisco: Jossey Bass.

Livingston, G. (2014, December 22). Fewer than half of U.S. kids today live in a "traditional family." Pew Research Center. Retrieved November 5, 2018, from pewresearch.org.

Livingston, G. (2018, April 27). About one-third of U.S. children are living with an unmarried parent. Pew Research Center. Retrieved November 5, 2018, from pewresearch.org

Lynch, R. F., & Werner, T. J. (1992). *Continuous improvement: Teams and tools.* Atlanta, GA: QualTeam.

McEwan, E. K. (1992). *Solving school problems: Kindergarten through middle school.* Wheaton, IL: Harold Shaw.

McEwan, E. K. (2002). *10 traits of highly effective teachers: How to hire, coach, and mentor successful teachers.* Thousand Oaks, CA: Corwin.

McEwan, E. K. (2003). *10 traits of highly effective principals: From good to great performance.* Thousand Oaks, CA: Corwin.

McEwan, E. K. (2006). *How to survive and thrive in the first three weeks of school.* Thousand Oaks, CA: Corwin.

Morgan, R. (2003). *Calming upset customers: Staying effective during unpleasant situations*. Menlo Park, CA: Crisp Publications.

Overby, T. (1613). As quoted in What does put your best foot forward mean? (n.d.). *Phrase and idiom dictionary*. Retrieved April 18, 2019, from http://www.writingexplained.org

Palmer, P. J. (1998). *The courage to teach: Exploring the inner landscape of a teacher's life*. San Francisco: Jossey-Bass.

Peck, M. S. (1978). *The road less traveled*. New York: Simon & Schuster.

Persell, C. H., & Cookson, P. W., Jr. (1982). The effective principal in action. In National Association of Secondary School Principals (Ed.), *The effective principal* (pp. 22–29). Reston, VA: Editor.

Rosen, M. I. (1998). *Thank you for being such a pain: Spiritual guidance for dealing with difficult people*. New York: Three Rivers Press.

Rowe, M. P. (1990). Barriers to equality: The power of subtle discrimination to maintain unequal opportunity. *Employee Responsibilities and Rights Journal, 3*(2), 153–163.

Scott, S. (2002). *Fierce conversations: Achieving success at work and in life one conversation at a time*. New York: Viking.

Senge, P., Kleiner, A., Roberts, C., Ross, R. B., & Smith, B. J. (Eds.). (1994). *The fifth discipline fieldbook: Strategies and tools for building a learning organization*. Garden City, NY: Doubleday.

Spacey, J. (2017, November 16). *6 types of relational capital*. Retrieved November 12, 2018, from simplicable.com

Tavris, C. (1978). *Anger: The misunderstood emotion*. New York: Simon & Schuster.

Taylor, G., & Wilson, R. (1997). *Helping angry people: A short-term structured model for pastoral counselors*. Vancouver, BC, Canada: Regent College.

The Dalai Lama. (n.d.). Spiritual quotations. Retrieved December 4, 2018, from http://www.spirtualityandpractice.com/quotes/quotations/view/16469/spiritual quotations

Variable. (n.d.). *Business dictionary*. Retrieved December 25, 2018, from http://www.businessdictionary.com/definition/variable.html

INDEX

Confident Teachers, Inspired Learners

GRAVITY GOLDBERG

In *Teach Like Yourself*, Gravity Goldberg applies ideas from fields of psychology, education, and science to name five key habits involving core beliefs, practice, relationships, professional growth, and one's whole self.

SERENA PARISER

This handy guide offers 50 proven best practices for managing today's classroom, complete with just-in-time tools and relatable teacher-to-teacher anecdotes and advice.

VICTORIA LENTFER

Whether you're new to teaching, working with at-risk students, or simply looking for new strategies, the CALM method provides an actionable framework for redirecting student behavior.

LISA WESTMAN

Full of step-by-step guidance, this book shows you how to build collaborative student-teacher relationships and incorporate student voice and choice in the process of planning for student-driven differentiation.

To order your copies, visit corwin.com

No matter where you are in your professional journey, Corwin aims to ease the many demands teachers face on a daily basis with accessible strategies that benefit ALL learners. Through research-based, high-quality content, we offer practical guidance on a wide range of topics, including curriculum planning, learning frameworks, classroom design and management, and much more. Our books, videos, consulting, and online resources are developed by renowned educators and designed for easy implementation that will provide tangible results for you and your students.

CAITLIN KRAUSE

Mindful by Design provides 24 detailed exercises for teachers and students, including step-by-step mindfulness lessons embedded into specific curriculum areas, ready to implement immediately.

JOHN ANTONETTI AND TERRI STICE

Use the Powerful Task Rubric for Designing Student Work to analyze, design, and refine engaging tasks of learning.

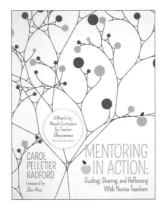

CAROL PELLETIER RADFORD

This newly revised workbook-style resource provides a robust companion website featuring videos, downloadable forms, and a digital Mentor Planning Guide and Journal for reflection.

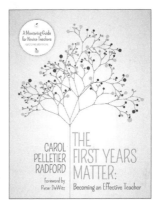

CAROL PELLETIER RADFORD

This second edition prepares new teachers for the rigors and expectations of the classroom and includes mentor-teacher strategies, a flexible twelve-month curriculum, companion website, and more!

A SAGE Publishing Company

Helping educators make the greatest impact

CORWIN HAS ONE MISSION: to enhance education through intentional professional learning.

We build long-term relationships with our authors, educators, clients, and associations who partner with us to develop and continuously improve the best evidence-based practices that establish and support lifelong learning.